My Pathway to Paradise

Shirley Zillig

I dedicate this book to my husband and the love of my life, Bob Zillig. Without his encouragement, I would not have accomplished so many things. I also dedicate it to my children and their families.

Acknowledgements

I truly believe I would not have what I have today without God's blessing on my life. He has been so good to me, and I thank Him every day.

My precious husband, Bob comes next on my list of whom to thank. We were eighteen and twenty-four when we were married, and we grew together over decades of wedded bliss.

My mother and father were also a great blessing to me. My dad was a true mentor, and my mother was a delight to have around. Their love for each other carried into my own marriage, and for that I am grateful.

Mammie Altman, my maternal grandmother, was my childhood playmate, and I cherished her as I grew to womanhood.

I wish my brother Vernon, was here to share this with me. Marm, my brother's wife, is the sister I never had. I am so glad to call her my friend.

My precious daughter, Bonnie, shared a passion for flying. I will never forget our times together in the cockpit. Linda and her husband Jack spent many years in Guam where both their sons were born. I'm so happy they live close to me now. My daughter, Chrissie and her husband, John own a home in the country with a pond, a dream of hers since childhood. Like me, she has realized many of her dreams.

Steven, our youngest, took over the reins of the Jiffy-tite business and ran with it. I am so proud of his accomplishments.

I dearly love my children's spouses: Laird, Archie, Jack, John, and Barbie.

My dear friend, Evie DeStefano (Nee Nucherino) and I have known each other since we worked together in my father's office in 1942. I cherish our lifelong friendship.

I feel my life is complete since moving into assisted living complexes. I have made many friends, and I appreciate everything the staff does for me.

Evelyn Miracle (her real last name), took on the task of putting my story on paper. I am amazed at how she jogged my memory during our time together. Her writing skill makes my story a joy to read.

TABLE OF CONTENTS

Preface

I have led a blessed life in my eighty plus years. Dancer, wife, mother, businesswoman, grandmother, sailor, pilot—these are all my titles. I did things that others could not or would not try to do, because I never gave up on my dreams.

Married to a wonderful man for 64 years, our philosophy was to give sixty percent and expect forty percent in return. I knew if I made my husband happy, happiness would be returned to me. As we enjoyed decades of wedded bliss, we raised four children, became grandparents to thirteen grandchildren and eleven great grandchildren. I wrote this book for them as well as the many others that urged me to write the story of my life. As I document my own history, I hope it inspires others to find their own pathway to paradise.

Showbiz, Here I Come

My breath came shorter as I took one last look in the mirror in my dressing room. Mother stood behind me brushing invisible lint from my costume and fooling with my hair. It was 1936, and I was about to perform for the first time as a professional dancer.

"Do I look okay?" I asked my mother. "Do you think I look old enough?"

"Shirley, you and Doris both look perfect. You'll knock 'em dead," Mother said beaming. I was practically hyperventilating. At age eleven I was passing for an eighteen-year old dancer at a small tavern in Buffalo, New York. The rouge and lipstick added to my already mature features. I hoped the manager didn't figure out that I was really too young to be dancing at his place.

"I'm so excited!" said Doris, my dance partner. "Our first real job in show biz."

I could hear the band playing a jazzy tune. In just a few seconds they would finish playing, and we would tap our way onstage.

"Five minutes, girls." The stage hand knocked on our dressing room door to let us know we were on next.

"Aren't you forgetting something?" Mother held up my tap shoes. In all the excitement I had forgotten to change my shoes.

"I'm so nervous," I said as I fastened the straps. "I hope I don't forget any steps."

"Come on, Shirley. You don't have anything to be nervous about," Doris said. "You know the routine inside and out,"

"Don't forget to smile." Mother pushed me out the door and over to the stage entrance. We had already given the three-piece band our music and run through the number a couple times that afternoon.

The clinking of glasses and the buzz of conversation died down as the master of ceremonies announced our act. Almost like magic my feet began to move to the sounds of the music and my arms followed suit. There was no need for mother to remind me to smile. I was having the time of my life.

Grand Debut

Dancing onto a stage in 1936 was not the first time I made a grand entrance. My arrival on May 14, 1925 was quite a production too. Before I go any further, I must set the stage by going back a few generations.

The love story of my maternal great grandparents, Marie Wehrle and Peter Bowen took place in the pre Civil War years when canal boats were still the best method of transportation in western New York. My great great grandfather Wehrle, a German immigrant, owned and operated several barges on the Erie Canal, although I do not know the exact location.

Passengers rode on the boats pulled along by horses, mules, or oxen. The Erie Canal, stretching 363 miles from Buffalo to Albany, was a modern marvel when it was completed in 1825. It linked New York City's harbor on the Atlantic to land west of the Appalachian Mountains before the advent of the railroads. It was affordable transportation and offered a way to get produce to market more quickly. It was also a lot more comfortable than riding a stagecoach for hours or days on end.

According to the story, my great grandmother, Marie, fell in the canal one day. Perhaps her big hoop skirt tripped her, but whatever the reason, she fell into the water. It must have been a struggle to stay afloat with the heavy, wet skirt and petticoats. One of the young deck hands, Peter Bowen, rescued Marie. She wouldn't give him the time of day until his heroic act won her heart. They were married about 1854 and had ten children. I met

3

Rose Bowen (Mammie), age 16, 1888

Great Grandmother Marie Bowen when I was still a young child. She died just one month shy of her 100th birthday in 1936.

My grandmother, Rose, or Mammie as I called her, was one of the Bowen's ten children. Born in 1874, she grew up and married Frank Xavier Altmann in 1891. At the age of 18, my grandfather started working at Mr. George Pierce's factory on Hanover Street in Buffalo. The company produced bicycles, birdcages and ice boxes. Early in the twentieth century, they started manufacturing cars and changed their name to The Pierce Arrow Motor Company. Grandpa Frank transferred to the plant on Elmwood Avenue in Buffalo where he made gasoline tanks for the cars. He never learned how to operate the cars he helped build, so he relied on his daughters to drive him around.

Rose (Mammie) Altmann (laying down) with daughters Mildred, Loretta, and Mae, about 1914.

My grandparents had four children: Frankie, Mae, Mildred, and Lorreta.

My Mammie Altmann was a very loving and compassionate woman. Little Frankie was seriously injured in an accident when he was about eight years old. He was hospitalized for several years before he died, but my grandmother never missed a day visiting him. It didn't matter if the weather was sunny or blizzard conditions, she walked there every day.

My mother, Mildred, was the third child in their family. She was born in 1902, one year after the Pan American Exposition opened in Buffalo. Her interest in show business was evident even as a child. She would borrow her father's coat and hat and put on little plays for her parents.

"Papers for sale, papers for sale," she would say, playing the role of a corner newsboy. As she got older, she dreamed of becoming a dancer. In those days show business consisted of burlesque and vaudeville and did not have a good reputation, so her parents did not allow her to pursue her dreams. She decided if she ever had a daughter, she would let her take dancing lessons.

Mildred Altmann, 1920

The Henrys

My paternal grandparents, Clark and Verennia Henry, immigrated to the Buffalo area from Welland, Ontario, Canada about 1890. Both sides of my family had connections to great cars from the beginning. My grandfather, Clark, worked as a chauffeur for a wealthy family in the 1920s. While still in their teens, my father, Clarence and his brother, Charlie worked as mechanics for the Pierce Arrow Motor Company.

By the 1920s the beautiful Pierce Arrow cars were widely used by the rich and famous. They supplied cars for the White House and shipped them to members of nobility all over the world. Movie stars rode in them too.

Uncle Charlie Henry and my father, Clarence Henry; Aunt Mae, and my mother, Mildred

The automobile industry may be what brought my parents together. Perhaps one day my mother picked up my grandfather from work and met the young Clarence Henry who worked at the same factory. Whatever the circumstances, Mildred and Clarence met and fell in love. They had a June wedding in 1923 and lived with my maternal grandparents for about three years.

In May of 1925, my mother was in her tenth month of pregnancy carrying me. The doctor informed my parents that Mother needed a cesarean section, but there was another serious issue: I was only an inch from Mother's heart. The incision would have to be done differently than the standard procedure. My birth would be the first c-section done this way at Deaconess Hospital in Buffalo, New York; therefore a gallery of doctors witnessed the operation.

Rose (Mammie) Altmann with a Pierce Arrow car of the day.

If that wasn't enough to announce my arrival, I rode home in style. My maternal grandparents Frank and Rose Altmann, purchased a brand new Pierce Arrow automobile so my father could use it to drive me home. The price tag on those cars was upwards of $6,000, a lot of dough in the 1920s. Possibly Grandpa Frank got a great discount since he worked for the company. In any event, it was a fitting way to bring me home from the hospital.

Mammie and Frank Altmann on one of their annual trips to Atlantic City.

My parents were still living with Mammie and Grandpa Frank Altmann, and I immediately became the center of attention. My early childhood was filled with love and joy as I grew and took my first steps.

We celebrated my first birthday in May of 1926, but a few months later, my father experienced a great loss when a terrible drowning accident took the lives of his two younger brothers. One hot August day that summer, my Uncles Elmer and Amasa (Wyvette) Henry ages 19 and 21, attended an outing for a church youth group at Brant Beach on Lake Erie. The water of Lake Erie can quickly whip into big waves, and this beach at the mouth of Cattanauga Creek is known for its treacherous undertow. People swam there in spite of the posted warnings. According to newspaper reports, a large swell pulled the young people into deep water. Even the good swimmers found the undertow difficult to handle and many of the victims could not swim. Five people made it to shore, and a few others were rescued. The newspaper accounts reported ten lives lost that day, including one of the rescuers.

In addition to my two young uncles, the victims included two teenage sisters from one family and a brother and sister from another family. What started out as a fun day at the beach ended in tragedy.

I heard only snippets of this sad story as I grew up. With such a great loss, it's understandable that my father didn't want to talk about it.

Family photo taken between 1923 and 1926. Back row L to R:: My grandfather, Clark Henry; Uncle Charlie, and my father, Clarence Henry. Front row: Grandma Verennia Henry; my mother, Mildred; my Uncles Elmer and Wyvette Henry

Lollipops and Noodles

One of my earliest memories was visiting my Aunt Mae's mother-in-law, Mrs. Murphy, in the swanky Hotel Statler located at Niagara Square in Buffalo. Aunt Mae took me there when I was about three. In those days, it was not unusual for wealthy people to live in a high-high-class hotel. However, the hotel businessman, Mr. E.M. Statler had plans to build hotels that would be affordable to the average traveler. His innovative ideas were very successful, and his company built a chain of hotels in big cities across the country.

Aunt Mae on her wedding day, circa 1920s

The nineteen-story Hotel Statler, completed in 1923, boasted many firsts in hotel design. It had things like private bathrooms with bathtubs, hot and cold running water, a wall light switch for every room, and a radio in each apartment. The building was said to be the largest in the state outside of New York City. With structures like this, Mr. Statler certainly earned his distinction as the Father of the American Hotel.

The lobby of the hotel was decorated with huge potted palms and comfortable chairs.

We ate lunch in the big dining room with its beautiful, domed atrium and linen tablecloths. Aunt Mae ordered a club sandwich and a chocolate milkshake for me. I called them toothpick sandwiches because they were held together with fancy toothpicks. It was all very fancy to a little girl.

Mother had another child when I was only two, but my baby brother only lived twelve hours. I was

A picture of me, about age 3.

thrilled when another baby brother, Vernon, came along when I was four. With the family growing, we moved into our own apartment above a shoemaker's shop.

The neighborhood offered a world of wonders for me. An Italian family, the Friesas, owned the shop downstairs. Wonderful smells came wafting up the stairs to our apartment. I went downstairs daily and knocked on their door to ask if I could eat there. Mother dressed me nicely thinking I was invited. I was too young to realize I was lying about the invitation, and everyone seemed happy.

When I showed up, I looked too adorable to resist and Mrs. Friesa loved feeding me. Homemade spaghetti from their kitchen became my favorite. I made lots of visits at the dinner hour until one day Mrs. Freisa mentioned to my mother how cute it was when I came to visit. That was the end of my free-loading on the neighbors, but I still love spaghetti.

Another great place was the bakery next door. The aroma of fresh bread and cinnamon rolls often lured me over there. The baker would give me a bowl of the sweet, whipped-cream filling they put in the donuts.

Across the street from the shoemaker shop was the ice cream parlor and candy store owned by my father's parents, Clark and Verennia Henry. My mother worked for them, so I had all the vanilla ice cream cones and lollipops I could eat.

My Uncle Roy and I

Uncle Roy Henry and me in front of the ice cream shop

Clark and Verennia Henry

would sit out in front of the shop and eat ice cream cones. He was just a few years older than me.

My father worked as a test pilot for Consolidated Aircraft in Buffalo when I was very young. He met Larry Bell there who was a fellow employee. When Consolidated moved to California, Larry started his own company, Bell Aircraft, and my father went to work for him as a mechanic. Dad could do anything he set his hand to: mechanics, cooking, and even sewing. He took on many household tasks as his younger siblings grew up, probably due to his father's declining health. When America entered World War I in 1917, his brother, Charlie, was called up. My father's care of the family precluded his service in the war, so he served his family instead. The years of cooking and sewing for them gave him a wide range of skills he used all his life.

My parents had a very affectionate relationship. They were always hugging and kissing and called each other Hon and Babe. It rubbed off on me, too. We practically hugged each other goodbye when we took out the trash.

When I was about four, we visited my paternal great grandparents, Albert and Minerva Henry, at their farm in Welland, Ontario, north of Toronto. My parents and grandparents and my Uncle Roy drove up there on mostly dirt roads. The cars were open at that time, so it was a pretty dusty ride.

My grandparents, Clark and Verennia Henry, my Uncle Roy, my mother and me on our visit to the farm.

We stopped at a roadside stand to buy a five-cent glass of buttermilk. I learned to love the thick, tangy stuff, and to this day I always keep buttermilk in my refrigerator.

I watched Grandpa Henry milk the cows, and sometimes he would shoot the milk right into my mouth. I didn't even care

when he missed and the warm milk trickled down my chin. I wished we could visit them more often.

At the age of 52, doctors told my Grandpa Clark Henry he would only live a few months unless he moved to a warmer climate. He took the warning seriously, and they moved to St. Petersburg in 1930. The change in climate did wonders for his health, and he lived another sixteen years. Their move to Florida paved the way for a southern migration later by my parents and Bob and I as well.

Hail, Hail, the Gang's All Here

I spent most of my childhood at our home on Tacoma Avenue in a suburb of Buffalo. The neighborhood was well supplied with a grocery store, a meat market, and a couple of drug stores. Dozens of children lived there too, so I had lots of friends to play with. In those days kids played outside until dinnertime. We played ball and jacks, hide and seek, or hopscotch.

We were also known for our funeral parades. If a bug or caterpillar died, we put it in a matchbox and headed for the empty lot in the neighborhood. As we walked along we sang, "The worms crawl in, the worms crawl out, the worms crawl over your nose and mouth." Then we buried the tiny box in our makeshift graveyard.

The attic at the Tacoma Avenue house was my personal playroom. I had a doll crib, a table and chairs and all my toys. I played by myself for hours up there, and my little brother was not allowed. Luckily for me there were plenty of boys his age in the neighborhood, so he had playmates to keep him busy.

On Saturdays two or three of us gathered around the radio at 11:00 to listen to "Let's Pretend", a half-hour program dramatizing Grimm's Fairy Tales. The program opened with, "Hello Pretenders," from the host, and the audience responded, "Hello Uncle Bill." I listened to stories like Rapunzel or Jack In the Beanstalk. The sponsor for the program was Cream of

Wheat, so the host gave plugs for the hot cereal at the beginning, middle and end of the program. In the evenings, the whole family sat around listening to radio programs like Fibber McGee and Molly.

Since television hadn't made its debut, people had to use their imaginations while listening to the radio. Sound effects played an important role in capturing audiences. Sounds of galloping horses or a squeaky door opening conjured up mental images of the action. It was a far cry from today's special effects, but it was every bit as entertaining to me.

Although radio occupied our time at home, we enjoyed going to the Saturday matinee at the North Park Theater. We paid twenty-five cents to watch the weekly serials, short movies with cliffhangers at the end. We wanted to come back the next week to see what happened. On Friday nights, the theater lured adults by offering a plate or cup and saucer with their tickets. Mother collected a whole set of dinnerware that way.

One of my favorite movie characters was Tarzan. I wanted to live in a tree house in the African jungle like Tarzan and Jane. I imagined swinging through the trees and calling out with Tarzan's famous yell.

Of course, I can't leave out Shirley Temple, a wonderful child star whose first movie came out in 1932. Everybody loved her. She could tap dance and sing, and she had the cutest head of curls. Just like movie stars of today, her image was marketed with plenty of clothes and toys. Mothers copied the Shirley Temple hairstyle on their little girls. I remember playing with a set of Shirley Temple paper dolls.

In the summertime we practically lived outside. We played games on the sidewalk, went for walks or rode our bikes all over town. Sometimes I rode my bike several miles to my cousin, Ruth's house in the city. She had the most beautiful dollhouse her father built for her. It was five feet long and three feet high. The rooms even had lights in them. We loved playing with that. If we got hungry, we might run out into the garden in the backyard and dig up some carrots and potatoes. We washed them off and sat under the porch eating them, enjoying the cool, dark space. I later heard that eating raw potatoes wasn't good for you, but I guess it didn't hurt me.

Mammie and Grandpa Altmann lived next door to the Schmidt family. Their son, Bob played the piano, and sometimes he accompanied me as I practiced tap dancing. Bob changed his last name to Smith and became famous a few years later. He started out as a singer and had a popular kids' radio show in Buffalo. He went on to host a TV show in the fifties with a marionette named Howdy Doody. His TV character, Buffalo Bob, always started the show with the question, "What time is it?" The kids in the audience, known as the peanut gallery, answered by singing, "It's Howdy Doody Time, it's Howdy Doody time." His successful thirteen-year run on television assured Buffalo Bob a permanent spot in American culture. Today his Howdy Doody puppet holds a cherished place at the Smithsonian, but I knew Bob when Howdy Doody was just a piece of wood in somebody's workshop.

Swimming in Lake Erie was a favorite summer activity as I was growing up. Our family drove about an hour and a half to Empire Beach on the Canadian side of the lake, our favorite place to go. We drove onto the beach, parked two cars together, and draped a blanket between them to create some shade. It was a great place for a picnic lunch.

When I was eight or nine, several of my school chums from P.S. 81 formed a club. I would call up area businesses and ask if we could come for a tour. Then we rode our bikes there. We went to Kittinger Manufacturing and saw how they built furniture. Another time we went to an ice warehouse to see how they cut the big blocks of ice.

In those days people used ice boxes to keep food cold. The ice company kept the ice in straw and delivered it house to house with a wagon or truck. The ice man would grab the huge brick of ice with big, black tongs and carry it to our door every day. It was a big event when we got an electric refrigerator.

I rode my bike over to my grandparents' house quite often. Mammie Altmann had tea parties with me. As the first grandchild, I was very favored. Mammie would make bread and every now and then she would playfully slap me in the face with the dough. Grandpa Altmann was mostly in the background. He was a jolly, rotund man. He was so proud of the X. initial of his middle name, Xavier, and he made sure everyone knew about it.

Mammie saved up for a baby grand player piano. She showed me how to put rolls of music on it and we sat there pumping and singing along as it played. Besides playing the piano, Mammie showed me how to clean the ivory keys with milk. She explained the enzyme in milk took the yellow out of the ivory.

When I got a little older, my friends, my brother and I used to take turns jumping off the roof of my grandparents' garage. A telephone pole with iron rungs provided a convenient ladder with which to climb. I'm sure Mammie scolded us for such dangerous behavior, but to my recollection, nobody ever broke a bone.

Halloween in the neighborhood was fun. Sometimes we would go to the meat market and get chicken feet. It sounds funny, but it was free fun for us. We would pull on the tendons of the chicken feet to make the claws move. Pretty good prop for Halloween! Trick or treating in that neighborhood and time was always safe for kids.

Sometimes we took chicken feet to the bus stop and waited. When the bus driver opened the door, we would throw the chicken feet in. Another mischievous thing we did was pick up potatoes from an outdoor grocery stand. We waited on a corner and shoved the potatoes into the exhaust pipes of cars at the stoplight. When the light turned green, the potato came flying out with a loud pouf.

Wintertime included taking the big toboggan we had over to Delaware Park. I liked riding down the hill, but I didn't like getting cold. We wore wool coats and those mittens that have a string that goes through your coat sleeves. Scarves and hats topped off the cold-weather outfits, so we looked like pudgy mummies. After being out in the snow for a while, the wool got soggy and smelled bad. My toes and fingertips burned with the cold.

Vernon Henry

One time when my brother was about four years old, he was all bundled up as we always were in the wintertime. He had on a heavy jacket with a hood, but he also wore a cap under the hood. Somebody hit him on the head with a brick, and he came crying to me. I helped him inside and tried to calm him down. Mother took the hood off and saw the bloody mess. She was so squeamish at the sight that she went to pieces. Even though I was just a kid myself, I took a wet cloth and softened the dried blood. In order to do a thorough job, I cut Vern's hair a little bit. My experience giving first-aid to my brother made me dream about becoming a nurse someday.

I remember the terrible elixir Dad sold door to door. It was called Helpalax. Whenever we saw Mother with that pint-size bottle and a big spoon, my brother and I scurried under the beds to hide. It was the vilest, brown stuff I ever tasted. I don't suppose Dad had any repeat orders which is why he didn't sell it for long.

We stayed pretty healthy in spite of all the diseases that were around at the time. Vern and I both had measles, but never whooping cough or tuberculosis, which were prevalent then. Vernon got scarlet fever once, so the house was quarantined. My dad and I stayed with my grandparents for three weeks. We took food over to our house and left it in the vestibule for Mother and Vern. I could see her at the top of the stairs through the glass in the door. We could have short conversations through the door and then we had to leave. I was so glad when they lifted the quarantine.

Christmas in the Sunshine City

We usually spent the holidays with Mammie and Grandpa Altmann. One Christmas I found coal and onions in my stocking. I cried because I didn't think I was naughty enough for such punishment. It was really a joke, and my grandparents felt badly that I got so upset. They compensated with a huge box, but they told me it was full of shoestrings. When I opened it, I saw a three-foot tall, beautiful doll. She was so big I dressed her in children's clothes. I named her Shoe-strings because of the joke, and she became my favorite.

Mother and Dad decided to visit his parents in Florida for the Christmas of 1932. Father's sister, Alphretta, and his brother, Uncle Charlie, went with us, too. The trip seemed to take forever. Cars didn't go very fast back then, and there were no interstate highways. I'm sure I didn't like being close to my pesky little brother for so many hours. I don't remember what games Vern and I played on the way, but we saw some interesting sights.

During the late twenties, Burma Shave shaving cream signs began to appear. These red signs with white lettering came in sets of six. Each sign had one line to a jingle, with the Burma Shave logo at the end of the series of signs.

As we traveled into the southern states, we saw a lot of cotton fields. Another familiar sight along the roads back then was the chain gangs. Each prisoner wore a black-and-white -striped uniform and ankle shackles chained to a heavy, iron ball. Guards with guns stood by watching the men as they worked alongside the road. This was a pretty scary sight for an eight-year-old.

We took rest stops along the way, but there were no fast food places to drive through. We would stop for gas and eat at a diner, or get sandwiches to take with us in the car.

Finally we arrived in Jacksonville to visit my father's sister, Viola and her family. It was so good to get out of the car. The next day we continued driving to St. Petersburg. We drove past many orange groves along the way. We stopped a few times to pick sugar cane from the fields to suck on.

My grandparents lived in a house built on short stilts on an unpaved street, Second Avenue. Every day a tall, black man came down the street wearing a top hat and white apron. "Fresh fish," he yelled. "I got 'em. Caught 'em alive. Come get your fresh fish." I don't remember eating fish, but that man hawking his wares made a lasting impression.

My mother and aunts walked down to the park every day to get their bottle of sulphur water from the Fountain of Youth. It smelled like rotten eggs, so I was not about to try it. I can't fault it though because they all lived into their 90s!

The St. Pete Times advertised free papers any day the sun didn't shine, but I don't think they gave away many papers. St. Petersburg certainly earned its nickname, The Sunshine City.

The famous green benches in the downtown area and in the parks became a symbol of St. Pete's hospitality. People could sit and enjoy the lovely weather on those benches.

My family in St. Petersburg, December 1932

Shopping in St. Petersburg left a lasting impression on me. We went to a huge drugstore known as Webb's City. Mr. James Webb, or "Doc" as he was called, bought his first drug store in 1925 and he continued to buy stores during the depression. He was a man ahead of his time, using the formula of stocking in bulk and selling at cut rates. Sam Walton used the same philosophy years later in his Walmart stores.

Doc Webb sold anything and everything in his stores. By the time we visited in 1932, his store encompassed several city blocks in St. Pete. I had never seen a store like it, yet one thing I saw created a question in my little mind. Why were there separate drinking fountains, one for whites and one for colored people?

The Million Dollar Pier extended about 3,000 feet into the Gulf of Mexico. It was completed in 1926, and it was a sight to behold. Trolleys brought people from the downtown area of St. Pete. Since it was Christmas time, all the palm trees leading out to the pier were decorated with lights. The trees looked like they were wearing glittering jewels. Decorations included life-size statues of the Nativity.

One day my father took me fishing on the pier. He gave me a little stick and a string with an open safety pin tied on the end. He probably didn't expect me to get anything, but I caught a little six-inch shiner. As my father took it off the safety-pin hook, a pelican came along and snatched it from us. After that I was not too interested in fishing.

Every evening at 7:00 the streetcars came by with children singing Christmas carols. A different school was represented each night and the driver was dressed as Santa Claus.

Christmas in the sunshine was a new experience for me, but I didn't miss the snow and cold one bit. All too soon it was time to get in the car for the long trip home. We waved goodbye to my grandparents, but I knew I would come back to Florida one day.

Vernon and I on a St. Pete beach

Shuffle off to Buffalo

When I was about five years old, Mother took me to an upstairs dance studio somewhere in Buffalo for my first dance lesson. She helped me tie the black ribbons on my shiny, patent leather tap shoes. Even though we were in the midst of The Great Depression in the early 1930s, my parents found money for lessons.

Our class learned a simple shuffle step while standing in place. Shuf-fle step. Shuf-fle step. Then we learned how to do it while counting to eight. I loved hearing the tap, tap sound as the metal on the soles of my shoes hit the floor.

A few lessons later I was flapping across the floor as my blond curls danced along. After that came flap, ball, change, another simple tap step. I was hooked. I took other types of dance lessons over the next several years, but tap remained my absolute favorite.

When I had been dancing for a while, my friends and I put on a show for the family and neighbors. We divided the garage into two sections, one for the performers and one for the audience. I not only danced, I staged the whole review. We did a dance to "The Lady in Red" and a few other numbers that we had on records. The show was a forerunner of things to come.

At eleven years old, I had become a very good dancer. My teacher, Mae Steck, had a daughter a little older than me who performed professionally. Mrs. Steck told my mother that she thought I was good enough to be in show business, too.

In those days, all the taverns had floor shows. Prohibition had been repealed in 1933. Now that alcohol was legal again, the supper clubs replaced the secret speak easies as they were called. The clubs offered a place for food, drink, music, and dancing. They needed entertainers, but I had a problem; performers had to be at least eighteen. However, that didn't stop my mother from looking for dancing jobs for me.

The year I started dancing professionally, 1936, the federal government initiated the Social Security program. I always loved the name Patricia, so I chose it for a stage name. Mother and I filled out the Social Security paperwork, making Patricia White the required eighteen years of age. Later on I changed my name back to Shirley Henry and kept the same Social Security number. I still got credit for all my years of dancing as Pat White.

That first dancing job was a sister act with my neighbor,

Doris. We danced at three places in Niagara Falls, New York, about twenty miles from Buffalo. The pay was $5 a night at each place. It was good money for the times, and I loved it. My mother would call booking agents and pretend she was me looking for dancing jobs. We started out doing shows only on the weekends and holidays. My mother and Doris' mother would drive and stay with us the entire night. Later on they dropped us off and came back at 3:00 in the morning to pick us up.

Doris and I did tap and soft-shoe numbers to popular music. We took our costumes in suitcases and went early enough to give the band our music so we could practice it a few times before the show.

My mother and father designed and sewed all my dance costumes. Usually I wore two-piece outfits with a skirt and blouse with ruffled sleeves. If I was doing a soft-shoe number, I might wear a long, flowing skirt with a big floppy hat like a Southern belle.

My favorite gown had a long, chartreuse skirt with a halter top. The skirt had accordion pleats with a red-sequined mid section. I also got into character dances such as Dutch, Hawaiian, or Gypsy. I danced in wooden shoes for the Dutch number, and wore a grass skirt for the hula. The Gypsy costume had long, chiffon strips of fabric with bangles hanging, and I carried a tambourine.

Besides my parents making costumes, my Uncle Al Rovall offered to help me with his talents. He was a piano player and arranged the music for the band at each club. He played for me as I practiced at home.

Before becoming a professional dancer, I never had an allowance. I wasn't used to having money, so Mother put it all in the bank. I didn't really need anything, so it worked out fine.

After a year of dancing professionally, I thought of something I wanted—a fur coat. I knew the only fur I could afford was skunk. Yes, that's right, SKUNK. It was actually an affordable and popular fur in the 30s.

I saved my money and finally had enough for the $110 price tag. I thought I looked swell wearing my black skunk coat. The knee-length fur kept me warm, but if it rained, it really stunk!

In the summertime we took the coat to N.L. Kaplan's, the main furriers in town. They used some form of dry cleaning and then put it in storage for the summer months. That coat lasted me for many years, long enough for my daughter, Chris to wear it. It still hangs in my closet today, with no hint of a skunky smell.

One of the dancing jobs Doris and I had was at a private stag party at the Automobile Club near the Buffalo Airport. It looked like a southern mansion, and there were a lot of big parties there. This one had several acts with the star of the show being a stripper.

I opened the curtain slightly to look out at the audience. There in the front row was the principal of the high school! He knew how old I was, but I knew he was about to see a stripper in this show. When it was our turn to go on, Doris and I looked at everyone in the audience and ignored the principal. He must have decided to keep our secret if we kept his, because he never said anything to us at school.

After several months of dancing with Doris, I decided to go solo. Doris was a nice girl, but she danced like a cow. She stomped her feet so hard I thought she would go right through the floor. I was getting calls to dance as a single, so I broke up the act and moved on.

When I was twelve, I was one of six girls chosen for a show in Bradford, Pennsylvania just south of New York. I boarded the Greyhound bus wearing a light-blue skirt and bolero with a large-rim, blue felt hat with a grosgrain ribbon tied under my chin. At the time I thought I looked at least twenty-one, but I must have looked like a laughing stock.

By today's standards, it would be dangerous to put a young girl on a bus to travel out of state. But the pre-World War II years was a naïve time in America.

The job in Pennsylvania was at the Rod and Gun Club, a very classy place. We danced there for a week, and I made a lot of new friends. It prepared me for what was to come a couple years later.

The summer I was fourteen, I was hired to work at Hanney's, a nightclub in Buffalo. Harold Wallace was the leader of their twelve-piece orchestra. There were always opening and closing numbers with the whole cast of the show. Besides performing, I did the hiring and firing of the acts during the fourteen weeks I worked there. We had singers and entertainers such as Frank Fontaine and Foster Brooks who later became a big-name comedian. I ordered costumes and props for all these numbers. It was a lot of responsibility for someone so young, but they thought I could handle it. In spite of that, I didn't get extra pay for doing the job.

By the time I was in high school, I had the show business lifestyle down pat. I went to school where I was an average student. Then I came home after school and took a nap. I got up to eat dinner at about 5:00 or 6:00, and headed out to my dancing jobs. By 2:00 or 3:00 a.m. I went home and to bed for a couple hours. In the morning I got up and started all over again. I don't remember ever falling asleep in class, and my grades never suffered. Although I missed football games and school dances, I

Picture taken in my teen years wearing an orange angora sweater mother had made for me.

didn't really miss the teen social life. I thrived in my dancing career.

My childhood dreams of being a nurse were long forgotten by this time. The only reason I wanted to be a nurse was so I could be a flight attendant. The nursing degree was a requirement back in those days. My mother poo pooed the idea saying, "Shirley, if you're a flight attendant you'll be on your feet all day." What did she think I was doing, dancing on my hands? Nevertheless, I forgot about nursing and flying and concentrated on dancing.

For my sixteenth birthday I wanted an unusual gift. I wished for an old car engine to tinker with. My parents must have thought it was inappropriate for a girl, especially one in show business, to have grease under her fingernails. They gave me girlie stuff instead. I would have to wait several years to add grease monkey to my list of achievements.

One weekend in December 1941, I was dancing at a nightclub as I usually did. Someone at the club made an announcement about the Japanese attacking Pearl Harbor in Hawaii. Nobody knew where Pearl Harbor was at the time. It took a few days for the news to sink in. People crowded around their radios that week, and before long our country was at war. Life changed drastically for the young men who went overseas to fight as well as those of us here at home.

Everyone pitched in during the war. We saved aluminum foil, string, and other things. Rationing became a normal part of our lives. Gasoline, sugar, butter, and even shoes were rationed.

Factories went into defense work, and many women joined the war effort by taking jobs. Rosie the Riveter was the iconic symbol of these ladies, and my mother was one of them. She went to work at Bell Aircraft in the stock room. My father was already working there as a supervisor.

My father had worked as a mechanic for most of his life, but he had one other job when I was younger. He worked for the Pinkerton Detective Agency in Rochester, New York. He lived in Rochester, but we took the train to visit him on the weekends. I later learned he was doing some type of under-cover work, but he never talked about it. Looking back I wonder if he was involved in events that led up to the war.

I continued dancing during the war, but I became weary of the nightclub environ-ment and their clientele. I never tired of dancing though. In fact, I would rather dance than eat. A union was being formed for dancers at that time, and I didn't want to join. It gave me a reason to quit show business.

Since I had no college plans, I started pestering my fa-ther to hire me to work at the Bell Aircraft credit union. I had taken some secretarial courses, so I could do shorthand and type. Every night at dinner my mother and I gave Dad the stare. Finally he gave in, but with a warning. "Remember, Shirley, you are not my daughter there. You are my employee."

A young woman named Evelyn Nucherino became my boss at the credit union. She took me under her wing, and we formed a wonderful working relationship. She became a life-long friend, even though I only worked there a short time.

I was only 17, but I felt like I had lived a lifetime in my dancing career. Now that I had a nine to five job, I looked forward to my free time. Maybe I would have time to date. I had been around so many drunken men, I wondered if there were any nice guys out there. I still hoped that someday I would have a special beau.

Shirley Meets Bob--Wowser!

I met the love of my life on a sparkling Christmas night in 1942, and my future was changed forever. I didn't date much during high school because of my dancing schedule. Working at Bell Aircraft gave me time for a social life, but I hadn't met anyone yet.

We were at my Aunt Loretta's house for Christmas dinner, and she got a call from her friend, Caroline whose nephew was looking for a date. I knew Caroline and her son, Al, but had never met her nephew. Aunt Loretta put me on the phone and Caroline introduced me to a young man named Bob Zillig. He worked at Bell Aircraft, too and was off work for the holidays. When Bob's aunt told him I was only 17, he groaned and said, "Oh no, a bobby soxer!" Young girls who swooned over singers like Frank Sinatra were called bobby soxers. Needless to say, Bob expected to see a little teenage girl when he met me. Boy, was he in for a surprise!

When Bob picked me up, I was wearing a burgundy velvet dress and the three-quarter-length, silver-fox jacket that I got for Christmas. Bobby soxer? Not even close! If anything I looked like a movie star. His eyes bugged out at the sight of me. He began to think I was too old for him and not the other way around. He was 24, but because he had worked second shift in a factory since he was 18, he was not really experienced at dating.

When I saw him at the bottom of the stairs, it took my breath away. He was so clean-cut and handsome. I was used to seeing the seedier side of life working in nightclubs, so it was a thrill to meet such a gentleman. I set my sights on him that night, and he was a "dead duck."

We went to Auf Wedersein, a restaurant that had a twelve-piece orchestra. We enjoyed dinner and dancing, and when he took me home he sweetly asked if he could kiss me goodnight. We went out the next night, and had a third date on New Year's Eve. A few other couples were going out with us, and we all dressed up for the formal occasion.

Buffalo is known for it's bad weather on New Year's Eve, and this one lived up to the reputation. We went through some cold, sleety weather to get to Kleinhan's Music Hall. I was coming down with a sore throat, so we stopped at a drugstore on the way to get something for it. We danced most of the night away, then went to an all-night diner for an early breakfast. We attended 5:00 mass at St. Anne's Catholic Church on Broadway, and Bob took me home. My dad was just getting up.

I went to bed to recuperate from the all-night party, but ended up sick for three weeks. Bob came to visit me every day. He would bring a teddy bear or some other little trinket for me. By the time I recovered, we were engaged, January 17 to be ex-

act. Bob always said, "I don't know what happened!" I do. I found something good and I was not about to let him get away.

When Bob asked for my hand in marriage, Dad answered, "Well, we've had her for 17 years and we'll be glad to get rid of her." Dad always had a great sense of humor. One reason I fell for Bob was because he was a sweet, funny man just like my father.

World War II raged on, but I was in love and floating along every day. I became useless at work because all I could think about was Bob.

We spent all our free time together. The hardships of the war didn't seem to phase us because we had each other. Gasoline rationing meant that we were limited in where we could go. Bob had a system though. He conserved gasoline by pushing the accelerator and then coasting. The only problem with that was

The sailboat Bob built in his parents' garage.

it took so long to get where we were going. He showed me how he did it, but I just wanted to hurry up and get there.

One of Bob's passions was sailing. When he was 16, his neighbors had a summer cottage in Wilson, New York on Lake Ontario. They had to

Bob sailing with my only competition, a girl named Grace he dated very briefly.

My glamour shot

take a boat to get from the mainland to the little island. Bob fell in love with sailing then. He built a sailboat in his parents' garage and took it up to Olcott, about 30 miles from his home. Bob's love of sailing inspired him to do whatever necessary to conserve gasoline.

Bob invited me to go sailing one summer weekend, and we brought my mother along. The sailboat was about a nineteen-footer with a center trunk for the keel. Any time we turned the boat, we had to climb over the center and duck under the boom. Even a two-inch wave would slosh over us. Mother said, "Oh my gosh, why do you have to sail in such a wet boat?"

Months went by and it didn't look like the war would be ending any time soon. We wanted so much to be together, so we went ahead and made wedding plans.

I bought my wedding gown for $75. It was ivory, slipper satin with long sleeves and a beautiful long train. I wore a chapel-length veil and carried white steppenovias. Because shoes were rationed two pair a year per person, I had to borrow a ration stamp from a friend to get my wedding shoes.

During the rehearsal, Bob was so nervous. I took control during the practice, as cool as can be. Wedding day was another matter. Bob looked so wonderful in his morning suit. I could hardly believe he was mine. All I could do was nod my head yes during the I dos.

We had a small reception for family and friends in my parents' finished-off basement. After the punch and cake, we donned our going away clothes and drove off in my dad's Plymouth. We spent the night in a Buffalo hotel, and when we arrived at the airport the next morning, a whole family entourage came to see us off.

A photographer snapped this picture of us in New York City and sold it to us.

Even though we were on our honeymoon, there were reminders that our country was at war. The stewardess instructed everyone to pull the window shades down for take off and landing. This would prevent possible spies on board from taking aerial pictures.

We arrived in New York City and checked into the Taft Hotel at Broadway and Seventh Avenue. Bob carried me across the threshold and we unpacked. I was a bit embarrassed that Bob hadn't brought any pajamas along, and I made him go shopping immediately to get a pair. My mother had given me a lovely two-piece negligee for my trousseau, and it came with strict instructions. "Shirley, this is to hang on your bedpost and should only to be worn in case of emergency," she explained. I'm sure I blushed at her advice.

It took me a while to realize we didn't have to wear pajamas, but I washed them every week anyway and hung them on the clothesline. I didn't want the neighbors to talk.

Bob had saved up money for our honeymoon, and we enjoyed seeing the sights of the city. The lights for the amusement park on Coney Island were turned off for the duration of the war. Even with the lights off and my eyes shut I didn't like the roller coasters. Riding in the steeplechase was more my speed. We sat astride brightly painted, life-size horses that raced on metal tracks.

The Rockettes of Radio City Music Hall were a must see in New York City. Within the building was a very unique area called the Quiet Room. All the walls and furnishings were black. Patrons were encouraged to sit and relax. It did the trick for me. I was amazed how peaceful I felt sitting there.

We also saw a Broadway Show, a real flea circus, and a prototype of a color television. A camera pointed at everyone who walked by the display. Even black and white television was in its infancy back then. Most families didn't own televisions, but Bob's sister worked for a doctor who had one. She used to babysit for his children sometimes. Bob and I would go over there to watch TV. One of the shows we saw on the tiny, nine-inch screen was the Texaco Talent Show with Milton Berle.

During the war all production of television equipment was stopped, and broadcasting was scaled back. In England it was stopped altogether until 1946. Radio still remained the main access for news and entertainment.

Following our New York City honeymoon, we settled into a one-bedroom, furnished apartment. It was located behind a butcher shop owned by our landlord. That connection provided us with a few extra pieces of meat aside from our rations. One day our milkman offered me some extra butter if I would

Me in front of our first apartment

give him a hug. Other women may have surrendered to the milkman's advances, but not me. Besides, he was old and pudgy, and couldn't hold a candle to my handsome husband.

Bob was still working at Bell Aircraft, and because it was a defense plant, he had a deferment from the draft.

Money was pretty tight for us, but we still managed to go to the movies every Saturday. The Shea's Theater in Buffalo was an ornately decorated building with a spectacular lobby. It was built in 1926 and patterned after European opera houses. Many stars graced the stage over the years. In the 40s it was used as a movie theater.

I usually dressed up and wore my silver-fox jacket when we went to the theater, and I felt like a movie star stepping out onto the red carpet. At least for a couple hours I could imagine living the high life.

In reality we were like most people during the war. We used things until they wore out, and if something broke, we fixed it. With Bob's background he was always good at that.

For example, we owned an old Buick that Bob had to nurse along. He broke the key off in the ignition one day, so he rigged up a switch under the dashboard to start the car. Finally he decided to sell it,

One of our first cars

so he took it to a car dealer in Buffalo. He needed transportation to get back home, so the salesman showed him around.

"We've got this old Chevy," the salesman said. Old was right! It had a crank like an old Model T and the accelerator was held together with a hanger. They were asking $5 for it because the battery was worth that.

Bob cranked it up and started home all the while thinking, *Shirley's going to kill me when she sees this junker*. He imagined taking me to Shea's Buffalo Theater in that old car, and he knew I would look ridiculous stepping out in my fur coat.

He had to come up with something quick before I saw the ugly rattletrap car. He had read an ad that promised $25 for any car that runs. That would do it. He would drive the car over there, collect the money, and I would be none the wiser.

Suddenly he heard a loud CLANK, but he ignored it and kept driving. He pulled over to a phone booth and called the dealer that offered the $25. That's when he noticed the crank had fallen off the car, and he couldn't start it. He used another dime to call his friend Nick to come and get him. He left it at the curb in front of the Havana Casino, a very fancy place, and planned to return later to get the car. I can't imagine what the clientele thought that night when they saw that piece of junk.

Bob and Nick went back the next morning to get the car, but it was gone. Figuring it had been towed, they went over to the police impound lot. Sure enough, there it was. Bob decided not to admit ownership of it and left it there.

In the meantime, the Buick dealer couldn't figure out how to start the car Bob had traded in. He had forgotten to tell them about the hidden switch, but a phone call straightened that out.

One Sunday morning months later as we ate breakfast a police car pulled up in front of our house. *I wonder what's wrong?* I thought.

When we opened the door, the officer exclaimed, "You don't know the trouble I had finding you! Did you own a 1932 Chevy?"

Bob was probably thinking about the junker at the impound lot. Maybe this man was here to collect a fine.

To our surprise, the officer went on. "I'll give you $25 for the car. I can use the motor in my boat."

Bob took the deal, got his $25, and I never did see that car.

The first Christmas Bob and I were together as a married couple marked an important anniversary—our first date the year before. Bob wanted to give me a special Christmas gift to mark the occasion. His eyes sparkled as he handed me a box. I couldn't imagine what it was, and I nervously untied the ribbon and opened the box. Ski clothes.

Let me pause here and make one thing clear—I HATE WINTER. In my opinion, cold is a four-letter word. As I mentioned in an earlier chapter, my fingers burned whenever I got cold. I felt like I had been frostbitten on one of Admiral Byrd's Arctic expeditions.

Yet here was my beloved husband, excited to share another of his favorite past times. Bob loved skiing almost as much as sailing. When he was a young man, he made skis out of the slats of an old barrel. He also encouraged me to borrow his sister's wool ski suit, skis, and boots a few times, but I never dreamed he would buy me a set. He probably spent $25 on everything, but that was way too much money for something I hoped would stay in the closet. I put on my best thank-you-honey smile and prayed he would forget about me using the gift until the spring thaw. No such luck.

With the first new snow following Christmas, we were on our way to Chestnut Ridge Park just outside Buffalo to go skiing. The slope was only about 100 feet high. I could ski down it all right, but there were no ski lifts at this place. I didn't have enough strength in my arms to herringbone up the hill on my skis. Bob would get behind me and head butt me up the hill like a billy goat. He dug his poles in, gave me a push, repositioned his skis, and butted me again. After three tedious trips up the hill, Bob resigned as head butter. I had to maneuver myself up the hill so I could ski, and of course, I had to enjoy it.

I decided to use my brains the next time he suggested skiing. I came up with a good excuse for not going. I said, "Honey, I'm afraid to go skiing. What if I'm pregnant and I fall or something? That wouldn't be good." Bob agreed with my reasoning, so my skis spent the winters in the closet. I wasn't far off in my pregnancy prediction either. The skis were long forgotten the following winter when I found out our first baby was on the way.

44

The Zilligs and Stegers

After I married a Zillig, I learned more about Bob's family background. Much like my ancestors, both sides of Bob's family were German immigrants. His paternal grandparents, George and Maria Zillig arrived in the Buffalo area in the 1870's where George worked as a picture-frame maker. He probably took what work he could get at first, but as opportunities opened up to him, he became a cabinet maker.

The Zilligs raised seven children, four sons and three daughters. George Zillig used his woodworking skills to design and build a mahogany cradle and completed it with ornate carvings. It rocked many Zillig babies as it was passed down from generation to generation. The cradle held each of our children, and after several years of storage, it rocked more Zillig descendants as we passed it on to our son.

Bob's father, Andrew was the sixth child born to George and Maria. Evidently he was quite a ham. This photo appeared in a Buffalo newspaper in 1905 with the caption, "Andrew M. Zilig, leading man in Alpheus Dramatic Club of Buffalo."

The Stegers

The men on Bob's maternal side of the family were tailors. His grandfather, Alois Steger, emigrated to America in 1873 and two years later married Rose Shoenberger. He carried on the family trade and opened a tailoring shop in Buffalo. With all the tailors in the family, it's no wonder Bob cut such a fine figure in his morning suit the day of our wedding.

Like the Zilligs, the Stegers had a large family. Bob's mother, Margaret Steger was born in 1891.

Margaret Steger, about 1895. The original photograph was a tintype.

L to R: Margaret,, Amelia (Mill), Caroline (Din), Henry, Hilda, Alois Steger and unknown man. About 1900.

Margaret as a young girl.

Andrew Zillig,
Bob's father

and had several younger siblings.

Andrew and Margaret were married in 1909. His brother, George Jr. had married Margaret's sister, Theresa in 1903.

Andrew's draft registration for World War I is dated September 1918, three months after Bob was born and two months before the war ended. Because of his late entry into military service, he probably did not go overseas.

Following the war, he worked as a bacteriologist for the Buffalo Health Department. Andrew was an intelligent man. While much research was being done on the disease of polio, he wrote a paper on the cause of it. Because he did not have a medical degree, he could not publish it.

Andrew's parents raised the family in the Catholic faith. Andrew's brother, Martin, became a Jesuit priest, and one sister became a nun, Sister Anastasia.

Father Martin, spent most of his life teaching. Prior to World War I, he taught at Georgetown University, Washington, D.C. He left for the Philippines in 1923 to teach at the Ateneo de Manila University. During the Japanese occupation of World War II, the school was severely damaged and many of the priests were imprisoned. Following the liberation of the Philippines by allied forces in early 1945, Martin boarded a ship for

California. He returned to the Buffalo area for a time to recover from his POW experience. I met him briefly that year when he gave a blessing to our first child, Bonnie. Father Martin later returned to the Philippines where he spent the remainder of his life.

The Zilligs in 1919.: Front row:Sister Anastasia; George, Maria, Father Martin. Andrew, Bob's father, is standing back row left.

Bob's Childhood

Bob grew up with two older sisters, Rita and Margie.

His mother doted on him, and he grew up to be quite spoiled. In my household, my parents and brother and I shared all the chores. When we were married, Bob had a big surprise. Our first dinner home as newlyweds, Bob discovered how different our families were. He got up from the dinner table, and I asked him, "Where are you going?"

"I'm going into the living room to read the paper," he answered.

"Oh no you're not. Your dishes are still on the table." From then on he was always helping.

Whenever my mother-in-law visited, she tried to overrule. If Bob was in the kitchen drying dishes, she would rip the towel from him and say, "Go in the living room where you belong."

Sharing responsibilities worked in our marriage, even though it was not the norm for families in the mid-twentieth century. Our ability to work together served us well throughout our married lives.

Pattycakes and Sparkle

I suspected I might be pregnant the summer of 1944, so I made an appointment with an obstetrician. Bob went with me, and we were thrilled when the doctor confirmed the pregnancy. In my excitement I forgot to zip the front of my dress after the exam, and walked into the waiting room with my slip showing.

Bob with pregnant me

A few months into my pregnancy we moved in with my parents. My doctor got Bob's draft deferment extended until the baby was born, but we were unsure how long the deferment would last. Eventually we knew Bob would be drafted and have to leave.

My parents fixed up a bedroom for the nursery, and my sister-in-law gave me a beautiful shower. I ate whatever I wanted during the pregnancy and gained a whopping 70 pounds. The baby was due in late March. Bob told me, "Honey, you can have the baby any time at all, but not April 1."

My parents, brother Vern, and me. The maternity fashions of the day always had a bow over the belly. This was taken early in my pregnancy.

Mammie Altmann was thrilled about the news. A week before the baby was born my mother called her. "Shirley had a little girl," she reported.

"No, she didn't!" Mammie replied.

Mother quit teasing and said, "You're right. She didn't have the baby yet."

I went into labor ten minutes after midnight on Easter Sunday, April 1. Bonnie was born eleven minutes to 11:00 and weighed seven pounds seven ounces. How's that for luck?

When Mother called Mammie to tell her the news, Mammie thought she was joking again. After all, it was April Fool's Day! My father got on the phone to convince Mammie we

Four generations: Me, Mother, Mammie and Bonnie

weren't fooling. I'll never forget that Easter dinner, wearing a corsage, sitting on a bedpan in a hospital bed after giving birth to my little girl.

Bob was so sweet seeing me go through child-birth. He told me, "Honey, I'll never do this to you again." But when I was ready to go home seven days later, he told the staff, "See you next year!"

Bonnie and I, Summer 1945

When Bonnie was just a couple months old, Bob's draft deferment was about to expire. He decided if he were going to be drafted, he would rather join the Merchant Marines. The ships carried supplies for the troops

and they were sitting ducks for the Germans. Even though it was high risk, Bob preferred it because of the pay of $1,000 a trip. He went in as a Chief because of his engineering experience at Bell Aircraft.

After 90 days of training he was to ship out of New York City in August. The war ended just a few days later, and he delayed going. I worried thinking the military police might come after him, so I convinced him to report to New York.

He was there a few days and found out the pay would now be $90 a month and his position would be an oiler. Bob told them, "I've got a family to support now. I can't live on $90 a month."

They threatened him saying, "If you leave now, you'll never ship out of the port of New York again." He never did, but that was fine with him. He came home to be with Bonnie and me.

Mother and Dad's home on Century Drive in Buffalo

With the war finally over, things were better for everyone. Bob had worked in factories so much as a young man he said he never wanted to do it again. He loved being outside. He came up with a business idea—delivering fresh eggs. He would visit the farmer's market early every morning and buy the eggs. Any cracked ones ended up in our refrigerator. I fed Bonnie the yolks only because at that time the doctors thought the whites were bad for babies. Rather than throw the egg whites away, I baked a lot of angel food cakes.

In 1946, my parents moved to Utica to help run my Uncle Gordon's automobile dealership. My brother was a senior in high school and wanted to stay in Buffalo to finish school. Since we were still living in my parents' home, we stayed there until Vernon graduated.

Daughter number two was due to arrive in June 1947. Father's Day was the 15th that year, and Bob's birthday was the 16th. I decided I would only buy one present and wrap it

Vernon

for Bob. The other gift would be our new baby. I just didn't know which day she would be born. Linda Diane became a beautiful Father's Day present, and Bob didn't care what he got for his birthday the next day.

That year we moved to Snyder, New York, another suburb of Buffalo. The house on Huxley Drive was a boring gray, so we had it painted fire-engine red. It was so red that when the painters came to work they would make a siren noise.

Bob and I painted all the interior rooms with Pittsburgh Paint. The colors we chose were so unusual that a representative from the paint company came to see how it looked. My kitchen was bright yellow with blue trim and we painted the living room dove gray with pink windowsills. Upstairs in the master bedroom we chose kelly green with pink trim. We painted another bedroom royal blue and yellow. The paint rep thought we had done a nice job with our decorating, but he didn't offer us any discounts for the future.

The egg business we started after the war was short lived. When Easter rolled around again, we couldn't compete with the big stores. Bob had another idea though. Ed Amen, a friend of Bob's, told him about his bleach business. Ed said it was a lucrative business because housewives didn't like carrying the heavy, glass gallon jugs back and forth from the store. Bob decided to give it a try.

He made a 500-gallon tank out of marine plywood in the basement of our home. Then he used hot road tar to seal the inside of it. Bob learned how to mix the right ratio of chemicals for household bleach. We recycled Coca Cola jugs from drugstores or anywhere else he could find them. We labeled our product Sparkle.

Bob bought a used panel truck to deliver jugs of Sparkle four days a week. On Fridays we mixed the bleach. Each week he traveled on one of his four routes. By the end of the month, the homemakers on the first route needed more of our bleach. This business was quite successful, and we did it for four years.

I loved being a mother. Whenever I nursed Linda, I let Bonnie lay down next to us and I would read her a story. Bonnie's vocabulary grew much faster than her understanding. As a toddler, she was proud to tell everyone she met, "My daddy is so strong he can throw the bull around." How embarrassed she was when, as a young lady, she learned what the statement really meant.

Bonnie as a toddler

When Bonnie was about three years old, she put my young parenting skills to the test. One day she boldly announced, "I'm running away." She set out walking down the sidewalk while I blamed myself and cried. Like most kids, Bonnie didn't get very far before I ran to her and brought her back. The next time she tried it, I had learned a thing or two.

"Let me help you pack," I said as I put a few of her things in a little suitcase. My reverse psychology worked, and she never tried to run away again.

Besides taking care of the girls, I cooked, sewed, and decorated our house. I paid $5 for an old treadle sewing machine I found at a thrift store. I kept it set up in my bedroom all the time, and I loved sewing for the girls. I made everything from little girls' dresses to Bob's shirts on that machine. I used it until my fourth child came along when I replaced it with an electric model.

Bob was always an attentive husband and did what he could to make my life easier. He loved tinkering. Bob used his engineering experience to fabricate a dryer for me in the basement of our house. I had a wringer washing machine and used a clothesline for drying. That was more difficult in the wintertime. The homemade dryer worked like a charm, even if it wasn't approved by Underwriter's Laboratories.

Bob started with a metal box about the size of a desk. He made a cylinder to go inside it and bought a washing machine motor. He rigged it up with a pulley and a light switch, and there was a small opening for a door. Down in the bottom he put a radiant heater. As it turned, the lint would hit the heater and I could hear it burn up—zzt, zzt. I used that homemade appliance for several years.

Bonnie and Linda grew quickly, and soon Linda was toddling around imitating everything her sister did. Bonnie had outgrown nap time, but Linda still needed hers. I put her to bed every afternoon. Little did I know, she and her friend next door would chat through the open bedroom windows. Sometimes Linda climbed out of her crib and snuck out of the house to join her friend in the back yard. I found them one day having a dirt-eating party.

One of our favorite hobbies at this time was going to real estate open houses. My mother-in-law would babysit while Bob and I went out. We drove through neighborhoods with beautiful homes for sale just to look around. As soon as we pulled up in front of an open house in our old jalopy, it was obvious we were not prospective buyers. Nobody paid any attention to us, but we didn't care. It was fun to dream. We hoped we would own a lovely, spacious home one day.

Because we didn't have a big bank account, Bob and I were always careful with our finances. Each week we parceled out our money in envelopes marked for various expenses. We rarely had any money leftover to use for our amusement. Some weekends my parents would come for a visit. After the war they had moved to Utica, 200 miles away, and went into business with my uncles in an auto dealership. One Friday night when they were visiting, Mother suggested we go out.

"I'll have to see if we have any extra money first," I told her.

"Why don't you figure it out on Sunday after we go out?" Mom suggested.

"Mother, if we don't have the money on Friday, we certainly won't have it on Sunday!"

Bob and I had the same philosophy with money. We thought very responsibly about it, and if we couldn't afford to buy something, we made do without it. I was so careful with our expenses that I bought one bar of soap at a time. Even though it was a better deal to buy three bars in a package, I only had enough money to buy one. By counting our pennies like that we met all of our bills.

Although we enjoyed our own little family, Bob realized I missed my parents. He didn't care for the long-distance phone bills either. We decided to sell the bleach business so we could move closer to the family. We packed up and I looked for a house near Utica while Bob finished up some work in Buffalo.

We found a lovely three-story farmhouse with a full basement and a big barn garage on a half acre of land near Barneveld, about twelve miles from Utica.

Once we were settled in, Bob decided to try a new business—rack jobbing. He built display shelves and installed them at grocery stores. The racks held all sorts of toiletries and other odds and ends. Bob split the profits with the store owners.

We did pretty well at this business for a while, but the time came when it didn't support us. Bob had to go back into factory work in the Utica area. I think we both cried the day he picked up his toolbox.

Although Bob didn't like his job, we enjoyed our home. In the evenings we sat on the big front porch and watched baseball games at the field across the road. That wasn't the only thing we watched from the porch. Every night at dusk hordes of bats flew by. I never liked the thought of bats flying around, so I stayed on the other side of the screen door to watch while Bob and the girls made fun of me. "Mommy's afraid of bats," they teased.

I finally got over my initial fear and learned to appreciate the bats for eating all the bugs. Mosquitoes never bothered us during the summer months.

One summer night I was sitting on the porch combing out Bonnie and Linda's hair after their baths. When I finished, I stuck the comb in the back of my hair for lack of a better place to put it. Then I settled back to watch the bats. Suddenly I felt something on my neck! I went crazy for a moment screaming and flailing my arms, trying to get the bat off of me.

When the comb fell at my feet I realized how silly I acted. The phantom bat was really the comb coming out of my hair and slipping down my neck. Creepy, but totally harmless.

Maybe it was the nightly bat migration that gave my brother the idea to have a Halloween party in 1951. We held several planning meetings to prepare and sent out invitations asking everyone to wear a costume and not talk when they arrived. We turned our house into a haunted mansion and set up a maze for the guests. We hung plastic spiders and strings from the ceiling. Eggshells on the floor created the sound of crackling bones. We used an electric distributor tester to create lightning. Vernon dressed as a hunchback, and his fiancé, Marlene came as a big-busted lady. I wore a scary mask and shroud, but Bob's costume beat us all. He came dressed as a pregnant woman!

Bob was a good sport when it came to Halloween. One year I dressed him up as a ballerina. I made a wig from a mop head and created fake eyelashes with heavy thread which I starched and curled around a pencil. I made a white satin tutu with a set of falsies inside. A homemade pair of ballerina slippers completed his costume. I darkened my face with food coloring and went dressed as an Indian.

When Bonnie was old enough to go to school, Linda thought she could do some big girl things too. She walked to the corner store where they kept pedal cars on display. Linda thought they were free for the taking, so she climbed on one and pedaled home. The store manager saw her ride away in the little car, and called to let me know. I waited in the driveway, and told her she couldn't keep the car. She had to turn the car around and pedal right back to the store. She didn't understand that reasoning, and the incident repeated itself a few more times. Each time I got a call, "Mrs. Zillig, Linda took a car again."

One day Linda picked some flowers from the neighbor's garden. Then she knocked on their door and tried to sell the lovely bouquet.

Another incident occurred around dinner time. Linda asked if she could have one of the big red apples in the bowl on the table. I told her no, it was too close to dinner. She ignored me and took the apple anyway. After sticking her finger in it, she put the apple back in the bowl, turning it around so the bruise didn't show. When I found it and confronted her with the apple, she said, "I was just feeling the apple and my finger fell in." I sent that story to Reader's Digest. Linda didn't think it was fair that I got $25 for the story, but she was punished.

After we moved closer to my parents, my father left my Uncle's auto dealership in Utica and started his own business in Rome, NY. Here I am posing with my mother and Mammie in front of a new Studebaker at my father's dealership.

Flower Girls and Dancers

When Bonnie and Linda were five and seven years old, my brother asked them to be flower girls in his wedding. They were thrilled and looked forward to every dress fitting. The week before the wedding, they were both sick with double pneumonia. Our doctor made house calls in those days, so he came every day to check on them and give a shot in the bottom. Vernon or Marlene called each day to find out how the girls were doing. We would all be disap-

Vernon and bride to be, Marlene

Flowergirls, Bonnie and Linda

pointed if they couldn't be in the wedding, and I knew how much they wanted to wear their beautiful flower girl dresses.

The wedding day arrived, and the girls were still not completely well. Against doctor's orders, I put the lovely dresses on them and bundled them up in my mother's

66

and my fur coats. They made it through the wedding and fully recovered later. I think every mother has had to answer the question, "How sick is too sick?" when it comes to participating in a big event.

Bonnie   Linda

Bonnie and Linda took dance lessons in Utica, and I decided I should open my own dance school. We converted a room into a studio with a mirror and a ballet bar. I went to Rochester to a take tests so I could be a qualified dance instructor, and I joined the Dance Masters of America. I advertised in the paper and charged fifty cents for each Saturday lesson. I bought a used, upright piano and hired a young girl named Evelyn to be our pianist.

Mother enjoyed making my costumes again. This time I would be a teacher, not a performer. I still looked great with short, little dance skirts that stood out with a stiff crinoline underneath. Mother made them in various colors.

I taught tap and ballet classes for both boys and girls. One class had six or seven little boys in it, and they all wanted

Me on recital night

Bob with the girls

to dance like Fred Astaire after only one lesson.

Bonnie and Linda became my helpers by dancing in front of the class. The boys gradually learned the steps for a country-themed routine, and we dressed them in blue-jean overalls and straw hats. We held the recital in June at the school in Holland Patent. They allowed me to use the auditorium if I donated money to the school milk fund.

* * *

When it came time for Linda to start kindergarten, she developed stomachaches on cue. Whenever the bus came, the pains started. As soon as the bus drove away, she was miraculously cured. Finally I knew I had to put an end to it. "I'm going to send you to school," I told her, "and if it kills you, I'll send your dead body." That settled it.

I found out later she learned a new trick once she made it to kindergarten. She gave the teacher excuses to see her older sister. When she arrived at Bonnie's class, she would wail, "I wanna go home!" I'm sure her teacher figured out what she was doing and put a stop to it.

While we lived in the Utica area, my brother and sister-in-law had their first child. Seeing my little nephew gave me the baby bug, and soon I was expecting our third child. I had no idea that something would happen to put my pregnancy in jeopardy.

Bob had been insulating the attic, and when he nailed the tongue and groove boards back down on the floor, he didn't realize it weakened the ceiling below him. One day while he was at work, the girls and I heard a huge crash. We ran upstairs to investigate. The ceiling in the girls' room had fallen in a heap of dust and rubble on top of the two twin beds and the crib where my nephew slept when I babysat. As we entered the room, I was horrified to find a sharp, three-foot piece of ceiling plaster lying in the crib. All I could think about was, *what if I had been babysitting? It certainly could have killed an infant.*

The emotional trauma of the scene threw me into premature labor. I didn't want to alarm my daughters, so I asked Bonnie to call her daddy and tell him, "You have to come home right now because Mommy is having a nervous breakdown." In reality, I feared I was having a miscarriage. After some explaining on the phone, Bob came home and we called the doctor. Thankfully my pains subsided in a few hours and I calmed down. Bob cleaned up the mess and somehow fixed the ceiling. We counted our blessings that no one was hurt.

For Easter that year we bought six live chicks for the girls. We didn't think the chicks would make it past the cute stage, but they surprised us. We kept them in a box in the kitchen, but we had to keep getting bigger boxes. When they outgrew the boxes, Bob got some chicken wire and built a pen outside. In spite of Bob's engineering skills, the chickens often found a way out. The neighbors would call and say, "Shirley, your chickens are out in the field again."

It turned out we had five roosters and one hen. I got an egg a day from her. By late October we killed the first rooster. Then one by one they lost their heads. I plucked their feathers and cooked each one. The hen was the last one, and we put her on our Thanksgiving menu. She was loaded with eggs, so I used them to make the stuffing. Aunt Loretta was the only one at the table who seemed shocked. "Oh my gosh, you're eating that chicken!" she said.

Two days after thanksgiving I went into labor and gave birth to our third daughter, Christine Anne. She was named after Bob's maiden Aunt Christine Zillig. Bob always called her Aunt Teen.

Chrissie

Since we were in a rural area, I didn't have access to an obstetrician like I did when we lived in Buffalo. Our family doctor delivered Chrissie, and I had a very difficult time with the breach birth and recovery. Always my prince, Bob helped me get back on my feet both emotionally and physically.

Chrissie's namesake, Christine Zillig

Bonnie was nine and Linda was seven when Chrissie was born, so I taught them both how to hold, bathe, and feed the baby. I knew someday while my back was turned they'd want to pick her up. This way they would do it right. In the morning they would dress her and bring her to me for a feeding. They loved being Mommy's helpers.

Although we loved living close to my family, it was rough financially. After four years in Utica, we decided to move back to the Buffalo area where there would be more job opportunities for Bob.

71

We found a lovely home on Fletcher Street in Tonawanda, and Bob got a job as a car salesman. One of the perks of that job was driving the demonstrators. Bob loved it. Cars became another of Bob's passions and we joined a sports car club.

One day I got a call from my folks. My Uncle Al at age 47 had a massive heart attack. I traveled to Utica for the funeral and stayed about a week to help the family. I was so glad to return home and Bob was happy to see me—real, real happy. A few weeks later I realized I was pregnant, but I was afraid to tell Bob. We hadn't planned on another baby, and I wasn't sure how he would take the news.

Whenever we had something serious to discuss, we waited until we were in bed with the lights off. I told him with the shock of Uncle Al's death I had lost track of my schedule. I was sorry, but I was pregnant. Bob said, "Let's just say it's the best thing that could happen." He put me at ease with his loving attitude, and we looked forward to this unplanned blessing.

Caring for my husband and three girls kept me busy during this pregnancy, but I didn't let that slow me down too much. In spite of my ever-growing belly, I participated in the car club activities.

Usually the wife takes a backseat while the husband works on cars. Not in our case. At one time we had a Porsche with a broken shifting fork for second gear. We put the rear end of the car on blocks and put the kids' toboggan under it. We removed the gearbox and took it to a service station with an arbor press for repair. When we got it back, we reinstalled it, finishing at 2:00 a.m. and doing a test run.

We were supposed to be at the Holland Hill Climb at 5:00 a.m. Cars would be timed to see who could do it the fastest. Bob was driving and I was helping with the timing at the finish line. I waited and started to wonder if he had gone over the side. He finally made it with no accidents. We spent all that time and money on the mechanics, but it was the wrong size tires Bob put on the car that cost him a place in rankings.

The car club held gymkhanas in school or shopping center parking lots. They had an event set up with bowling pins to mark the areas. You drove into one, backed into the other, and drove around into the next one.

Another timed event required the driver to go around in a perfect circle while the passenger held a string tied to a bowling pin in the center of the circle. If the driver veered off course, the pin would fall over. The passenger had to jump out and set the pin up again. After the driver completed the circle, he had to do it in reverse.

By this time my pregnancy was seven months along. I needed help just to get in the car. There was no way I could jump out to set up a fallen bowling pin. Bob steered like a pro, and I held onto the string. He completed the course frontwards and backwards without dropping the pin. I think my participation in the gymkhanas while I carried Steven marked him for life. He has always loved cars.

Another time we borrowed my sister-in-law, Margie's, VW bug for a slalom event. The driver had to be blindfolded

Zillig Car Collection

These are just a few of the cars we collected over a lifetime. We fell in love with the Citroens

This is the car Bob owned when we met.

We called this Porsche, the Skunk because of it's unique black and white design.

A Lotus

NSU Sport Prinz

Datsun 280Z

and the navigator had to direct him without touching him. Bob and I practiced our directions. "Go slow, a little bit more to the right." We had it down pat. *This will be a piece of cake*, I thought.

When the time came to actually do it, my directions came out more like, "Oh, ah, oh!" Under pressure my navigating fell apart.

Bob yelled, "What should I do?"

My sister-in-law watched from the sidelines and asked Bonnie, "Why are they going so slow?"

"He's blindfolded," came the reply.

"He's blindfolded in my car?!! Oh my God!"

Needless to say, we didn't win that event, and we never borrowed Margie's car again.

In the early 60s, Margie drove her little car to California. She became enamored with Lawrence Welk and his champagne music when his television show first aired. The Lawrence Welk Show ran for 30 years on ABC and made him an American icon for conservative music.

Margie thought if she moved to California she could be closer to Lawrence Welk, so she put an ad in the Buffalo paper looking for a traveling companion. She and her new friend, Celia, set out for Los Angeles in her VW bug. Margie did most of the driving, stopping every afternoon around 4:00 when the glare of the setting sun was too much for her. When she arrived in L.A. she found a place to live and made herself a permanent fixture in Lawrence Welk's TV audience. Proof of that frequency lies in the pictures of Margie taking a turn on the dance floor with the star as he often did with guests of the show.

Left: Margie at a party with Lawrence Welk.
Right: Dancing with the star of the show.

Margie even sidled her way into Lawrence Welk's social life. She was invited to picnics, weddings, and other events given by the show's cast. Much to Margie's disappointment, Lawrence Welk stayed married to the same woman for 61 years.

* * *

My next-door neighbor, Esther and I had a morning routine which included having coffee after the children were off to school. "Guess what," I said one day. "I'm pregnant."

She responded by saying, "Guess what. I'm pregnant too!" We compared dates and found out her baby was due just a few days before mine. I enjoyed having a friend close by with whom to share baby plans. The day I went into labor I almost didn't want to go to the hospital so I wouldn't upset Esther.

"I can't go now," I told Bob. "Esther will kill me if I have my baby before her."

"Get in the car," Bob insisted. I did beat her to the delivery room by a few hours, but she didn't hold it against me.

Bob and I were thrilled to see our newborn son, Steven Robert, born in July 1956. Just as Bob predicted, this baby, "was the best thing that could happen." After having three girls, Bob was bursting with pride over his newborn son. As we drove home with our little boy, Bob gave Steven his first driving lesson. "Now son, this is how you downshift." We both anticipated years of father/son bonding like this.

The Zilligs, 1956

Living the Country Life

With the family growing we decided to look for a home in the country. We found an old house on Lapp Road in Clarence Center, New York. It was so old the beams in the basement still had tree bark on them, and there was a pitcher pump in the front yard. When we looked at the house, a snake greeted us in

the overgrown grass at the back door. This is the country all right! I knew the kids were going to love this.

The house sat on an acre of land, part of a three-acre piece of property with a little creek running through it. Some neglected patches of raspberry and rhubarb came with the deal. One year we had an enormous garden. I hired a man to plow a section of ground for me. Instead of doing the 10 x 20 feet I asked for, he plowed a plot 100 x 50 feet. I did my best to fill it up.

I didn't know how prolific tomatoes are, so I put in 60 plants. I had tomatoes on top of tomatoes. I planted green peppers, onions and squash. I even tried growing Brussels sprouts. When the garden was ready to harvest, I realized I had to do something with all this bounty.

If it grew, I canned it. If I couldn't can it, I froze it. I even rented space at the Hobart cold storage in town. I cooked rhubarb into as many variations as possible until Bob was sick of rhubarb. I made spaghetti sauce, stewed tomatoes, and tomato juice.

My friend, Evelyn's, father had a farm and she brought over a lot of food, too. With the bushels of pickles she gave me, I made dill pickles, bread and butter pickles, and relish. I made jam, preserves, and juice from the big, purple grapes she gave us. Fortunately I loved doing those things, and stocking the pantry came in handy for our family of six.

The children didn't always appreciate vegetables, but I insisted they eat some. One night we had peas for dinner and Linda complained. I told her, "You have to eat one pea for every year old you are."

She looked at me with pleading eyes and asked, "Well can you peel them for me?"

As my garden grew, so did the kids. Pretty soon Steven was a toddler and into everything. One day I was flipping the mattress in the girls' room and Steven found some mothballs I'd put under there to freshen it up. They had deteriorated from original size, and to Steven they looked just like candy. He popped one into his mouth. I didn't know what to do, so I called the drug store. They told me, "Oh, no, that's poison!"

We lived six miles out in the country, and Bob was at work. How would the ambulance find us? When they arrived I climbed into the back with Steven. I kept patting his face because he wasn't moving. I was terrified. He laid on my lap, mesmerized by the lights and siren.

I phoned Bob and he met us at Children's Hospital in Kenmore where they pumped his little stomach. They wanted to keep him overnight, and being a mother I thought the nurse needed detailed instructions on how to care for my two year old. Bob gently ushered me out of the hospital explaining, "Honey, I think they know how to take care of him."

It wasn't long after that Steven tried eating the caulk from around the bathtub while I was giving him a bath. The operator at poison control practically knew me by name.

Aside from his antics with toxins, we had fun with our little boy. When he was napping, I would go outside and find a garter snake and put it in a drawer for him. When he'd wake up, I would say, "Steven, Mommy has a surprise for you," and I'd show him the little snake. Like most little boys, Steven liked reptiles. Once Steven and Chrissie got ahold of a toad. They were about to squeeze the life out of the poor thing before I rescued it from their pudgy little hands.

When Steven got a little bigger, we bought him a one-person, plastic boat for the creek. Even though the water was only six inches deep, I made him wear a life jacket. He would get in the boat and it would sink down to the bottom and not move.

In the wintertime the creek would overflow and freeze, coming up to the lower section of our yard. Chrissie got a pair of ice skates when she was seven and Steven was five. Bob and I called her Elvis Presley because her legs went all jiggly whenever she attempted to ice skate on the pond. She hung onto Steven slipping and sliding, pulling his hat askew. We would stand in the kitchen and laugh at the sight.

Bonnie loved climbing trees. One day Chrissie tried it too. She climbed up one of the big trees in our front yard, but got scared and wouldn't climb down. "You have to climb down," I said from the bottom of the tree.

"I can't climb down," she insisted.

My urging didn't convince her, and she stayed up there for hours. Her big sister had to climb the tree and help her down.

I was always concerned about the safety of my children. I liked the wide-open spaces of the country, but I believed in boundaries too. Chrissie was still quite little and wanted to play outside, so I tied a string around her waist and tethered her to the pitcher pump in the front yard. That way I knew she couldn't wander off. She confessed many years later that when I went back in the house, she wiggled right out of the string so she could play. She knew not to go far, and when she got tired, she put the string around her waist again and called, "Mommy, I'm ready to come in now."

Our fascination with sports cars continued, although we did more looking than buying. Bob really liked the Citroen, a French import. By looking at the car, it seemed the French had never seen a car before designing it. I told him I thought it looked like an ugly clam and I never wanted to own one.

He surprised me one day when he pulled up in front of our house in one of those ugly cars. When he tooted the horn, it went "eek, eek." I hoped he was just taking it for a ride, but then he said, "Oh, by the way, I bought it."

I didn't believe him until he showed me the sales slip. I was furious until he took me for a ride in it. It had a hydraulic suspension making it a very comfortable ride. Bob also explained what safe vehicles the Citroen's were. Bob won me over, and over the years we owned nine of them.

Years later we worked on our cars together at a friend's garage. Andre had a French car dealership near us, and he allowed us to use his metric tools. One day I went in to repair a leaky hydraulic line in our Citroen. Bob was too busy, so I set out to do it. I donned one of Bob's old, white dress shirts and packed a lunch. When I arrived at Andre's garage, he was pretty busy. I hung around for about an hour and asked if he would let me work on the car. He couldn't believe I would be doing the work. "Are you serious?" he asked, as he looked me up and down.

Andre showed me where to park the car, and I borrowed a creeper to slide under it. He told me exactly what to do to get to the part, gave me the tools I needed and went to lunch.

A customer came in just before Andre returned. He looked around for some help, but I was the only one there.

When Andre showed up, he said, "Shirley, is this man's car ready yet?" The look on the man's face was priceless.

I took a part over to the repair shop next door to Andre's, still wearing my greasy "daddy shirt." They tested the part and found it was okay. When I asked how much, the man said, "Lady, we should pay you to see a woman with grease up to her elbows!"

I worked all afternoon on the Citroen, and Bob came by after work with suppers for both of us. "Okay, honey," he said. "I'll take over now."

"No you won't," I said. "I know where every nut and bolt is on this car." Bob handed me tools while I worked. We finished the repair and drove away at 6:30 that night. I loved anything mechanical, and it gave Bob and I one more thing to do together.

Alley-Oop and Pepper

Our acreage on Lapp Road included a couple barns, one of which was equipped with stalls on the lower floor. It had concrete floors and a doorway out to a pasture. One winter Bonnie asked if we could board two horses from the riding school she attended. She would get free riding lessons out of the arrangement. Bonnie was already an experienced rider at thirteen and had taught eleven-year-old Linda to ride English style too. The girls would enjoy having horses at home. Besides, how much could a few bales of hay cost?

Pepper was a five-year-old gelding, named for his white coat with black spots. His attitude matched his name. Alley Oop, or Ooper as we called him, was a twenty-five-year-old, retired jumper with a lot of life left in him. He was a chestnut-colored, gentle giant, standing about sixteen hands high. Since Bonnie was the older, more experienced rider, she rode Pepper and Linda rode Ooper.

The girls were responsible for the horses' care, which included feeding lots of those bales of hay, hauling water since there was no spigot at the barn, and cleaning stalls. It was no small task for two middle schoolers. The girls got up at 5:00 a.m. to do the horse chores, and after dinner they had homework and more horse care.

On weekends they groomed the horses and went riding on the circular path in the pasture by the barn. Sometimes they enjoyed longer rides into the countryside. I'll let Linda tell you a story about one such ride:

Linda's Wild Ride

Whenever we went on long rides, Bonnie would be in front on Pepper. We picked and ate ripe apples directly off the tree branches at face height. The horses enjoyed taking a fresh apple or two from the ground and leaving their own apple pies behind. Since I was in the rear position of the caravan, my horse had to side-step Pepper's used apples.

The cows in the pasture stood just far enough back from the electric fence to watch us. Sometimes we tried petting the cows, despite their slimy noses and the plentiful flies buzzing around them.

One day I decided to take Ooper out by myself. Bonnie was by the barn doing chores. Rain had left the ground slightly damp and muddy. I had no problem on my solo ride until I ended the walk and headed back to the barn. Ooper stepped in a puddle, spooking him. With no warning, he let out a loud whinny, reared up on his hind legs and took off. I instinctively leaned forward and wrapped my arms around his neck, hanging on for dear life.

I was scared to death, but knew I had to calm the horse down and bring him to a stop. Ooper had a different idea. The more I pulled back on the reins, the faster he ran until he was in a dead run. I don't know who was more terrified, the horse or me. I gripped the horse's neck and yelled at the top of my lungs, "Bonnie! Help me! Help, Bonnieeee!"

Bonnie rescued me from perilous situations before, but this time I was on my own. Ooper was running too fast for Bonnie to catch up. She told me later that she witnessed the whole thing and was run-

ning madly screaming, "Linda!" all the way in a fruitless effort to save me.

As Ooper galloped toward the barn, I saw he was headed for a ten-foot-wide pine tree next to the road. I looked to the side and saw there were no cars coming. I hoped Ooper's instincts would not allow him to run into the tree, but I mentally prepared myself for plan B in case he didn't stop.

He didn't. At the last possible moment, I released my grip on Ooper's neck, took my feet out of the stirrups, and leaned to my left to slide off his back. I knew I had to roll to the left immediately to avoid Ooper's feet. As I hit the ground inches from the tree, Ooper made a hard right. Without missing a beat, he headed down the middle of the country road like a wild stallion.

Bonnie ran up to me still yelling, "Linda! Are you all right?" I told her I was fine, but instead of the sisterly hug I expected, she turned around and started running away from me screaming, "Ooper! Halt!" Oh yeah, I forgot the mad horse in the middle of the road.

Ooper was approaching our neighbor's house a half mile away. I watched in amazement as he finally slowed to a trot and then stopped, waiting as if nothing was wrong. When Bonnie caught up to Ooper, she checked him over for possible injuries but found none. When she got him back to the barn and removed his bridle, she noticed a small cut on his lip. Every time I pulled on the reins, it applied pressure to the cut and he ran faster. All ended well, but it left me wishing I could see the little bubble of thoughts above Ooper's head on that wild ride.

Linda wasn't the only one that experienced Ooper's wild side. One day he got away from me. I ran after him, grabbed his tail, and hung on until he stopped.

Another time he kicked Pepper, breaking the skin on his leg. When the vet came, it was dark, and I had to hold a lantern so he could see. Caring for these horses was more of a challenge than Bonnie ever imagined.

There was a limit to what I would pay for *free* riding lessons. When Pepper bit one of the girls, it was the end of the Zillig Stables. We sent the horses back where they came from.

Shirley's Accidental Crematorium

While we boarded the horses, we kept a big bag of oats in our basement. One day I found some baby mice in the bag of oats. I was sure the hairless, pink things would freeze down there.

I remembered the little, white bunny I had when I was eight years old. The bunny was accidentally left in its cage on the porch one night. I was shocked the next morning to discover my bunny had not survived the first freeze of the season. I didn't want any other animals to freeze on my watch, even if they were mice.

I took the baby mice upstairs and Steven asked, "How do we get mouse milk to feed them, Momma?" I put the mice on top of the bathroom light for warmth. This was an unfortunate rescue for the mice. They went way past warm all the way to cooked! I felt bad, but the cat enjoyed the roasted mice.

You would think I learned my lesson about rescuing animals, but one day I took some baby barn swallows inside. Again, I tried to warm them with the bathroom light. *This time I won't leave them as long and they will be fine,* I thought. I must have been distracted with the children, because a little while later the cat got a meal of roasted barn swallows.

With this track record, it's no surprise that my approach to another animal situation would be unusual. Bob brought home four kittens one day, one for each of the kids. They were cute and fuzzy, but when they started foaming at the mouth, it became evident the cats had distemper.

I had to do something to protect my children and put the kittens out of their misery. I thought of a humane way to do it. I put them in a cardboard box and cut a hole in the side of it. Then I set it next to our car's exhaust pipe in the garage and started the car. The kittens went to sleep permanently from the noxious fumes.

Kitty euthanasia is not politically correct by today's standards, but in the 50s, life in the country included some unpleasant tasks.

We had another kitten that I taught to be a mouser. She didn't have very good instincts. One day I saw a little mouse in the kitchen, so I grabbed the broom and swished the mouse toward the cat. At first she wasn't interested. I continued sweeping the mouse toward the cat until she saw it move and took her pouncing position. I picked her up and carried her out the back door with the mouse hanging from her mouth. After that, she often left presents for me at the back door.

One night we came home from an outing and saw a stainless-steel bowl overturned on the kitchen counter. A note next to it read, "Do not move this!" After questioning the babysitter and the kids, we found out there was a mole under the bowl. I don't know where they found it, but it was our job to take care of it. Bob gingerly removed the bowl and sicked the cat on it.

When we first moved to this house in the country, we felt we needed a guard dog for protection. The house was close to the road and it had big picture windows. Anybody that came onto the porch to our front door could look into the living room, making me feel quite vulnerable.

I always loved the old Rin Tin Tin movies, so we looked in the paper for a beautiful German shepherd like him. We found a dog named Duke who fit our qualifications. We bought a choke-chain collar to complete the guard-dog look.

It turned out Duke was a coward. If anybody came to the door, he would run and hide under the bed. After a few episodes like that, I grabbed his collar if I saw someone coming to the door. He would growl trying to get away. People thought I was holding him back from imminent attack. In reality, he just wanted to hide. It wasn't too long before we gave Duke his walking papers.

We replaced Duke with a mountain German shepherd. Tiny had a beautiful black coat and looked like a huge, fuzzy bear. Unfortunately Tiny lived up to his name. He was big in stature but short on watchdog skills.

We were struggling along financially at the time because Bob had been unemployed several months. He tried selling a concentrated shampoo door to door until he found a better job. He went out every day peddling the stuff, and we kept the money in our bedroom. When he came home one day, he noticed the money was missing. He asked me if I had moved it, and I told him no.

We couldn't figure out where the money went, so we called the police. We were shocked to learn there had been a string of robberies in the area. The prime suspect was a traveling sewing machine salesman. Evidently the suspect came by our house when we were gone. I was thankful none of the children were home from school when the robbery occurred.

It appeared the thief had little opposition when he came to our house. Just like his predecessor, Tiny was no watchdog. We went to bed that night devastated with the loss. Bob had no job and no prospects either. Now the little bit of money we had was gone. It was a low point in our lives, but I refused to give up. As we held each other that night, I encouraged my husband. "We are a family with four children. God isn't going to forsake us."

Shortly after that, Fred Koch, a realtor friend of ours came by. He asked what Bob was doing and I told him about our recent troubles.

"Tell him to come and see me tomorrow," Fred said. He put Bob to work doing odd jobs at first, and then worked him into selling real estate. It was the first rung of a ladder rising to new heights for us, and it would go higher than we ever imagined.

Let's Pretend

It would soon be time for our youngest to start Kindergarten. I explained the procedure of getting up and getting ready to Steven. At the end of my detailed description, I said, "The school bus will come and take you to school. Won't that be fun Steven?"

"No! I'm not going. Not unless you go with me," he replied.

"But Steven, I'll pack you a nice lunch. And you'll get to play with your friends on the playground every day. Won't that be nice?"

"Nope. I'm not going."

Steven continued his refusal, so during the summer before Kindergarten, we pretended to get ready for school every day.

"Time to get up, Steven," I'd say. "You're going to eat breakfast, then we will pack your lunch just like on a school day. Then it will be time to ride the bus."

Steven played along, but always insisted he was never going to go to school. I was getting weary of trying to convince him otherwise when finally the first day of school arrived. When the bright yellow school bus stopped in front of our house, out the door he went. "Bye!" was all he said.

I felt like a pair of pants he'd outgrown and tossed aside. He didn't need me after all of that. I swallowed a lump in my throat as I entered this new stage of motherhood, with all my kids in school.

There was plenty to keep me busy. I still loved sewing. I made all Bob's shirts and dresses for the girls and myself. When Steven was born, Bob insisted I get an electric sewing machine. It seemed like so much money, and I felt so guilty I almost took it back the first week. I took a tailoring class soon after and learned how to make coats and hats. My stash of fabric grew as I constantly watched the sales. If I wanted a particular material, I waited until they slashed the price down to $1.25 a yard.

My children thought I could make anything and do it in the blink of an eye. One night Bonnie asked for a pair of riding jodhpurs, which she needed the next day. With only a few hours to fulfill her request, I perused my substantial stash of fabric and found a nice brown corduroy. With a few modifications to a pants pattern I used for Bonnie, I cut out the legs and sewed up the pants in no time. She probably never gave it a second thought. Mother came through again.

When the girls were old enough to go to school dances, I used my sewing expertise to fashion prom dresses. The girls could pick out a style in a pattern book, and I could sketch the design. I made my own pattern and sewed it out of sheeting first.

One year Bonnie needed a dress and we couldn't afford the $35 for a store-bought gown. My sister-in-law had given me a bridesmaid dress some time before, so I cut it down for Bonnie's formal. As she was getting ready to go, the zipper split. With no time to fix the zipper, I sewed it shut by hand while she was wearing it. Bob thought it was a great idea to sew our daughter into her dress. "She won't get into any trouble that way," he said.

I answered him with, "Honey, she may be sewn into it, but the skirt can always come up." Bob hadn't thought about that. Bonnie probably turned purple with embarrassment.

I sewed a lot of costumes for the girls over the years too. They both were in water ballet, and they needed costumes for school plays as well.

Sewing for my little boy was another matter. I was forever patching the holes in Steven's pants where he wore out the knees. I even had to patch his snowsuit!

Any time I saw a group of kids playing in the house or in the dirt, Steven was on his knees. I used to think he would go down the aisle on his wedding day on his knees. Because he stayed on the floor so much, he liked eating down there too. But he didn't like his sandwich on a plate. I remember one day I wiped up the floor in one spot and put his sandwich there where he ate it.

My girls were becoming little homemakers, learning how to cook and sew like their mother. One morning Chrissie announced, "Mommy, I made breakfast for you—oatmeal. I followed the recipe."

When I came out in the kitchen I saw where the oatmeal had boiled over and left a white residue all over the stove. One taste explained it. She had used half a CUP of salt instead of half a teaspoon!

Linda had a different experience when she made a lemon pie one time. She followed all the directions on the box of pudding mix, and it made a thick enough filling. The only problem was she threw away the little flavor ball because she didn't know what it was. The pie looked good but had no flavor.

By this time Bonnie was practically grown up and in her last years of high school. She was a talented student, both in academics and athletics. She was a gymnast, a cheerleader, and an excellent swimmer.

Bonnie applied and was chosen to be an American Field Service exchange student and was scheduled to go to Japan for three months during the summer. Prior to departure, she took some Japanese lessons from her history teacher who had been an interpreter for the Navy during World War II. Bonnie learned enough Japanese so she could converse with the family she would be living with.

I had a terrible time finding things to send with Bonnie as presents for the family. Everything I looked at said, "Made in Japan." I settled on a few items I thought were very American—Jiffy Popcorn, maple sugar candy, and instant pudding. We helped her pack and put her on a bus bound for Vancouver, B.C. where she would board a jet for Tokyo.

After a six-day trip by bus, plane, and train, she arrived in the fishing village of Yaizu City, Japan, about 120 miles south of Tokyo. The difference in culture became shockingly obvious to our 17-year-old daughter as soon as she arrived. When she stepped off the train, the Japanese father gave her a compliment. "You have very nice milk tanks," he said.

Bonnie explained that in America that would be very rude. I think it would be rude in any country.

Whenever we got a letter from Bonnie, I took it to the hometown newspaper to share. The second week she was in Japan, she wrote, "I'm a pretty big hit here because I'm considered the authority on English, twisting, and Troy Donahue."

I wrote to Bonnie, of course, but I also tried to put her out of my mind so I could deal with her being 9,000 miles away. I knew if there was an emergency, we couldn't be there. She

missed her family and her steady boyfriend too. I was heartbroken when a letter came saying she was almost at her breaking point. There was nothing we could do but wait for her time in Japan to be over so she could come home. It was a difficult experience for her, but one she never regretted.

The pilot let us sit in the cockpit after the jet landed in Japan. Me, Bonnie, and granddaughter, Susan,

Years later she and her husband hosted a Japanese exchange student named Yoshiko. In 1990 an invitation came for Yoshiko's wedding. Bonnie, her daughter, Susan, and I traveled to Japan for the wedding, and it was a wonderful experience.

While Bonnie was an exchange student the summer of 1962,, she wrote her boyfriend, Laird and we would exchange letters. We could tell they were very much in love, and when she returned we were soon planning a wedding. Bob and I had just celebrated our 20th wedding anniversary, and now our first-born child was getting married. Our lives were changing in other ways too. We were on the threshold of a new business venture.

A Tite Little Gadget

Even after Bob took the job with Fred, we still scraped by to pay our bills. Bob was selling real estate, and I got my license too so I could help out, but we weren't making much money. Bob knew we would do better if we had our own business again. The wheels were always turning in Bob's mind. He wanted to find something innovative that we could produce and sell, but what could it be?

As he pondered several ideas, he took a job with the Jack Kolberg Company as a sales representative for Hansen Quick Connects. The product was a brass quick-connector for the plastics and dye cast industry. The mold bases were in two big pieces of steel which had water lines going through them like a radiator to keep the injected plastic cooling at a certain speed and temperature. The Hansen connectors were used to feed the water through the molds.

Bob's job was to get accounts from companies that had previously turned them down, so he had a strike against him before he even opened his mouth. Hansen connectors were cumbersome, only came in one size, and only had straight hose stems.

Bob was always tinkering on things. He created a garden hose connector and he would give them to the purchasing executives in the factories he visited. It was a great door opener for him as a salesman, and they always asked for a couple more the next time he came by.

Selling his connector out of stores was a different story. He tried putting them in a few places on consignment, but shoppers didn't know or care what it was and walked by. Bob had tried selling other things in this manner and didn't like the results. He didn't give up on his ideas though. He kept wondering, *what can I do with this concept on a different scale?* Bob wanted to design something that could be used in industrial tool manufacturing where the market was much bigger.

After about six months, he was fired from Kolberg with the words, "You'll never be a salesman." Even though Bob got the axe, he had gained some valuable information. In talking with the purchasing executives at various companies, he asked why they didn't like the brass couplers he was selling.

"They're too bulky. They need to get around angles and into hard places," were some of the comments he heard.

Bob took the information he learned to his makeshift office in our musty, old basement. He had a little desk and a lamp down there, but no engineering stuff or drawing boards. All he had was a ruler and a pencil.

The atmosphere was not very conducive to creative thought either. Bob shared his office with our huge octopus furnace as we called it. Sometimes he would go down there in the middle of the night and a little garter snake greeted him with its head sticking out of the limestone wall.

Bob started working on a coupler using the dimensions he got from talking with the factory people. The average fitting was an inch and a half or more in diameter, but Bob designed his to be only a half inch in diameter.. He found out what size opening the factories wanted through the center, and he started with that.

Another complaint he had heard was that the male part of the connector stuck up from the mold surface. That meant they had to take it out to preserve it until they needed that mold for the next run. What good is a quick connect that you have to take apart and put back in the die every time you run it? Bob countersunk the hole and put the female plug into it. There was no protrusion when they changed molds.

Once Bob had all these ideas on paper, he made a prototype. He went to his friend, Bill Wheaton, who had a metal lathe, and made a connector out of brass. Then he made up a one-sheet and set out to sell his idea. We had no money to invest to get this thing off the ground, so he started taking orders with a delivery time three months away. It wasn't hard to get the orders. They practically grabbed it out of his hand. "I was looking for something like that," they would say. Bob got $1,000 worth of orders this way.

One place Bob visited was Eastman Kodak. He spoke with the purchasing manager as he had done at other companies. He looked at what Bob showed him politely and explained that the engineers at Hansen were working on the problem with the fittings. They were trying to design something that would only project half an inch over the mold.

"Well Mr. ___," Bob said, "Here's my answer to that." Then he showed him the little plastic thing and the connector he brought. "When you pull it off there's no projection."

"Do you have a little time?" the manager asked. "I'd like to introduce you to our chief engineer."

After he got some orders, Bob went to Curtis Screw. He didn't know anyone there, but he was hoping to find a company that would work with him. "What I'd like to do is have you produce this form," he said. "But you'd have to understand that I don't have any money right now. You'll have to wait until I get all of these things together and deliver the orders. Then I can pay you." Curtis Screw got on board, and then Bob went to four or five other companies to get the rest of the parts for his design.

Bob was a nobody from Clarence Center, New York. How did these manufacturers know we would actually deliver a product and that we would still be in business in six months? The product sold itself because it was such a good idea, but they were leery to give us a shot. Both Bob and I were excited with every order we got.

Our little Jiffy-tite company went into production in the basement of our old house in the country. We put all the parts together by hand, just the two of us at first. We often took champagne breaks to fuel our enthusiasm for the work.

We met our first batch of orders and took most of the profit to build up our stock. Bob got to know which connectors would sell the most and built up the business in those areas.

He went to the bank for a business loan, and they were impressed with what we had done so far. They questioned Bob about the market for Jiffy-tite connectors. "The product looks great, but once a guy buys this and puts it on his machine, will he want to buy more?"

"There's such a field out there, and nobody has what we have," Bob answered.

The first bank we went to turned us down, so Bob went to M & T Bank. This was the same banker Bob went to when he was unemployed and struggling to pay our bills. "Curt, I'm stuck," he had said. "I just can't make the mortgage payment."

"Don't worry about it, Bob. I'm glad you came in to tell me. Most people would just let it slide and avoid you. I know you're going to make good."

We did get back there in about three months to make up our payments. We appreciated what Curt did for us, and now that he was President of the bank, Bob went to ask him for a $5,000 loan. They drew up the papers and we got our loan. While Bob was there, Curt told him a story we never forgot, The Businessman's Story:

Two college graduates are back for a ten-year reunion. These two fellows were roommates, and one was really a knucklehead. He had trouble with math and just about everything else too. His roommate was one of these whizzes who could just put the book under his pillow and had it all together in the morning. He was a gem. He helped his friend get through school. So they meet and Harry says, "Little Joe, how are ya? It's nice to see you. How are you making out?"

"Boy, I'm doing great. I'm a college professor now and I teach math. I make about $32,000 a year. Things are going well. How are you doing, Harry?"

Harry says, "Things are going pretty good for me. I've got a home in Florida, an apartment in New York, and a place in Switzerland. I have a yacht, an airplane, and a Rolls Royce."

"What do you do, Harry?" Joe asks.

"Well, I invented this gadget. It costs me a nickel to make it and I sell it for a dollar. I know I'm only making 5%, but the money just keeps rolling in!"

That's how we got started in business. When we got the Eastman Kodak order, we hired Bonnie to work for us.

Things were going well, but Bob realized we couldn't keep this up. How could he travel around taking orders and be home to put them together too? Another problem was getting in to see the right people at the companies Bob visited. They would tell him, "So and so is very busy, so stop in the next time you're in town and we'll give you an order." Who knows when the next time would be? Bob found out the customers didn't want to wait months for an order. They wanted something that was already on the shelf.

The question arose, "Why don't you have a distributor?" Some of Bob's contacts recommended he contact DME, Detroit Mold Engineering. This company sold molds to manufacturers and it was right in line with what we were doing. Bob wasn't thrilled with the idea of giving up his profit margin, but after he thought about it for a while, he realized it was the right thing to do.

DME was a big company, and it wouldn't be easy to get our foot in the door. Bob started by telling DME who our customers were in Detroit so they could check out how people liked the Jiffy-tite product. It didn't hurt that the President of DME was a sailor too. Bob used that common ground to form a relationship. The executives at DME seemed to like what they saw, but they didn't give us a decision right away.

In the meantime, we looked into another company for distributing Jiffy-tite. National Tool had DME beat in the Northeast, but that is because they were concentrating in one area whereas DME served the whole country and Canada too. Bob had trouble getting in to see anybody at National Tool, so he went to Moog, a company just taking off in the motion technology industry in East Aurora, New York. They thought we had a terrific product, and they invited Bob to go to the Chicago Tool Show in November of 1963. Bob set up a Jiffy-tite display at the show, and he saw the DME representative while he was there. "What are you doing over there with Moog?" he asked Bob. "Come and see me tomorrow."

Bob took the meeting. "Bob, we're gonna go for it. Stop at DME in Detroit on your way home, and they'll give you an order," the rep told him. Bob was thrilled when it turned out to be a $10,000 order! Not only that, Bob knew that wherever DME went in business, Jiffy-tite would be there, too. It was a huge door opener for us.

Bob told them we would need three months to put the order together, and by that time we could keep up with their demand for product. With the order in hand, Bob called me before heading home. "Honey, I think we've made it!"

Bob crossed the bridge through Windsor and traveled across Ontario to Buffalo. At the border, the Canadian customs agent asked Bob a shocking question, "Did you know your President has been shot?"

Bob went from the emotional high of getting a huge order to hearing of the assassination of President Kennedy on the same day, November 22, 1963. We were thrilled to have the business breakthrough we needed, but saddened with the great loss of our President.

As the country mourned, we geared up to fill our biggest Jiffy-tite order to date.

Moving On Up

Even with no contract between DME and Jiffy-tite, our business out grew the basement of our old country home. The house had been up for sale for a few years with no bites, when suddenly we had a buyer. Selling our house now was timely, but it required we move immediately.

We asked the movers to come and give us an estimate. When they asked us where we were going, Bob answered, "We don't know yet. Just follow us and we will lead you to the new place." That was on a Monday and we were supposed to be out by Friday.

We found a two-story colonial in the Green Valley Subdivision in Clarence, New York. We signed the papers on the kitchen table at midnight on a Tuesday night, and were ready to move by Friday as planned.

Bonnie's wedding date had to be sandwiched in with the move. Our neighbors graciously offered their home for the wedding and reception. I don't know how, but we managed to pull off a wedding, pack our things, and make the move in record time.

Bob walks Bonnie down the aisle

Before long we had the Jiffy-tite shop set up in the bigger basement of

Bonnie and Laird

the new place. Since we had stepped up our production, Bob designed and built a machine to help us assemble the parts. He called it the winding machine. He constructed it from a washing machine motor and hinges from the back door.

Bob made a pass-through opening from the basement into the garage to make it easier to move the

boxes. Each 12 x 12 box held 100 connectors, with ten boxes in a carton. We loaded the boxes in our Citroen station wagon and it would sink down lower and lower with the weight. We never seemed to overload it

Our family, 1963

though because the hydraulic suspension in the car compensated for the weight. With each load, we made a trip to the Consolidated Freight Company in Tonawanda to ship the boxes to DME in Detroit.

Our partnership with DME was a benefit to both sides. They were going into companies in Europe looking for sales.

Everywhere they went, Jiffy-tite went, too. Our connector was a door opener for them because they could show it to prospective clients as something new and innovative. The "small peanut," as Bob put it, helped DME sell their bigger merchandise too.

We knew we had a good product because our suppliers gave us quality parts. Bob later learned that GM, one of DME's customers, had done time studies. They found out that using Jiffy-tite connectors saved thirty-seven minutes during every mold change.

In the past when they used pipe-thread fittings and hose clamps, the union required the set-up man call a plumber. They would have to wait for him to show up. With the Jiffy-tite connectors, the set up man could do every-

Straight, forty-five, and ninety-degree hose stems

thing because it didn't require a tool. Another big benefit to the mold manufacturers was that there was no leakage with our connectors as there had been with the old hose clamp system.

Bob and I went with DME representatives to a lot of shows for the plastics industry. Our product became well known and widely used among those companies.

As our relationship with DME grew, we decided to give a formal banquet in Detroit. I did all the set up from our home in New York. I booked the ballroom, planned the menu and color scheme, and made name tags. I memorized all the names of the guests and introduced the couples to each other like I had known them all my life. Even though they were from the same company, they had never socialized like this.

At the banquet we hosted in Detroit. Left to right: Frank and Phyllis Marra, President of DME; Bob and I, Sherm Crawford; Steve Pituck and wife. Steve was the DME purchasing agent we dealt with.

I was the perfect hostess. It turned out to be a beautiful event. We were so thankful for DME's business partnership, and we were happy to celebrate it with them.

As time went on during the sixties, the Japanese were making huge inroads in manufacturing. We began to worry how our business would be affected if they got ahold of our design. Would they come up with something similar? Would they put us out of business?

The executives at DME had clients in Japan by then, and they put our minds at ease. "They love Jiffy-tite over there!" they told us. Knowing our little gadget had gone global was really exciting, and it seemed we wouldn't be in competition with the Japanese after all.

Business was not the only expansion happening for the Zilligs. Our first grandchild arrived the same year we got the DME order. Bonnie worked for us throughout her pregnancy.

Whenever my parents visited from Utica, we put them to work too. It was truly a family business.

One day we were at the high school making pizzas for the annual fundraiser for American Field Service, the organization that sent Bonnie to Japan as an exchange student. Bonnie was helping out too. To our surprise, she went into early labor. We rushed her to the hospital and she delivered little David. He was two months premature and weighed only three pounds, nine ounces. Bonnie and Laird barely saw him before they whisked him off to another hospital with a preemie ward.

They put David in a special incubator. It was amazing to see such a tiny, little thing through the windows of the nursery. Bob looked at David and said, "He moves just like a real baby!"

Bonnie came home empty handed while the hospital staff cared for her baby. He would have to weigh five pounds before he could come home.

One afternoon as I was fixing dinner, Bonnie asked, "How big was he Mom?"

I held up the chicken I was preparing for dinner. "Well, Bonnie, this chicken weighs five pounds. So he was littler than this." Ever since then, I called David my little chickie. He calls me even now and says, "This is your chickie calling."

Bob used to say, "The worst part about being a grandfather was that he had to sleep with a grandmother." He didn't have too much to complain about since I was only 39 when I became a grandmother.

David had a lot of physical challenges and had several surgeries on his feet and legs. He is such an overcomer, not letting anything stand in his way. When he grew up, he got a job with IBM. He told me he didn't have a window in his cubicle office. I found a picture that mimicked a window and gave it to him. Pretty soon word got around, he had an office with a window. Some of his co-workers wondered how he managed that.

As the years clicked by, our business outgrew our basement once again. We did a major remodel by literally jacking up the bedroom area of the house and creating a new ground floor for the business.

Bathing and doing the dishes while our house was in construction mode was a real challenge, but it was worth the effort to keep everything under one roof.

Don't Call Us

With Bonnie grown and married, daughter Linda was next in line to leave the nest. She had been corresponding with Jack, a young man in the Air Force. When he got a chance, he took several military hops across the country from California to Stewart Air Force Base in New York and hitchhiked 360 miles to Buffalo to meet her. They hit it off when they met in person. He was later stationed at Montauk Point at the tip of Long Island, New York. He drove the 500 miles every chance he got so he could see Linda, but we limited him to one visit a month.

Linda was finishing her schooling in data processing at the time. When she signed up for her classes, I remember asking her, "What the heck is data processing? What will you ever do with that?" If anyone had told me in the future I would use a computer every day, I wouldn't have believed it.

In the fall of 1965 Linda and Jack were engaged, and we started planning another wedding. I offered my wedding gown

Linda and Jack's wedding, 1966

to Linda. It looked as beautiful as I remembered 23 years earlier.

Sunshine greeted us the morning of the wedding, Saturday, January 29, 1966. Linda looked lovely as she walked down the aisle on Bob's arm. It was the first wedding in the new Catholic Church in Williamsville, New York. The ceremony and reception were beautiful, and soon it was time to offer my last bits of advice to the newlyweds. "You're on your honeymoon now," I said. "Enjoy your time alone, and whatever you do, don't call us in the middle of the night."

I was referring to a sleepover Linda had as a young girl a few years earlier. She called us crying at 3:00 in the morning. Her dad got out of bed to go get her. I was teasing her, but I had no idea those words of advice would soon cause me much grief.

Linda and Jack stayed in Buffalo that night. About 9:00, there was a knock at Bonnie and Laird's door. "What are you doing here?" Bonnie asked.

"We came over to play bridge," Linda answered.

It seemed like a funny thing to do on your wedding night.

Sunday morning Linda and Jack loaded up their Karmann-Ghia and started out. Just like Bob and I, they planned to honeymoon in New York City.

By this time, blizzard warnings were out. We were somewhat concerned with the newlyweds traveling, but Jack knew the roads well after driving the route so many times. Surely the main roads would be plowed and they would be fine. What we didn't know was that Jack decided to avoid the New York State Thru-Way. He thought it didn't save any time and cost $15 in tolls.

Jack monitored the storm warnings on the radio, and he expected Linda, who grew up in the area, to know which counties were mentioned for severe weather. Although Linda is skilled in many areas, geography isn't one of them. Jack thought he was driving away from the worst of the storm, but in reality he was driving into the teeth of a record-breaking blizzard.

As the hours passed, we watched television news reports about the storm. We waited by the phone, hoping Jack and Linda would call. No call came. Here is Jack's account of what happened while we waited to hear from them.

As Sunday progressed, snow continued to build up on the road. We experienced whiteouts where the road, the land, and the sky all blended into one white visual field except for the highest tips of power poles. I used them as a guide to stay in the middle of the road. At one point I couldn't see anything, so I stopped the car to check our position. I had driven into the other lane, but there was no oncoming traffic, so we were fine. Suddenly an eighteen-wheeler zoomed by, missing our car by inches. Once I calmed myself down, I realized it was a blessing. I followed the truck, driving in its tracks for several miles.

We lost our guide when the truck pulled over into a truck stop. We continued driving using the power poles as guides again. With the gathering darkness, and the snow at least a foot deep, I pulled over to check our position. As I slowed to a stop, the car went off the road. We were stuck. The strong winds drove the snow horizontally. A police car with lights flashing drove by us, but didn't stop. I proceeded to dig the snow away from the car by hand, but I soon realized I needed a better method. I used my trusty pocketknife to remove the rear license plate, and it became my snow shovel. I dug the snow from all four wheels and tried driving out of the drift. It didn't work. I let the car run a few minutes while I sat with Linda to warm up.

My second attempt to dig us out failed as well. On my third try, I decided to dig twice as much with a break to warm up. The old saying about the futility of shoveling snow in a snowstorm is true. I was frustrated to see that the places I had just cleared were covered already. Our last option was to sit in the car with the motor running as long as we could since I couldn't dig us out. I cleared the snow away from the exhaust pipe, but I remembered the police car. Maybe if I could find him, we could get some help. Without telling Linda where I was going, I started off on foot.

The officer was stuck, too, but he had a radio. A tow truck arrived at the same time I did. Dave, the tow truck driver pulled the police car out of the snow, and I asked if he could pull us out, too. I pointed to our car's lights in the distance. I jumped into the cab of Dave's truck, and we passed three other cars stuck on the opposite side of the road. Once he freed the car and took his $10 fee, I followed him into town riding in his tire tracks.

We were out of the snow, but we had to find a place to stay. Trapped motorists overran the town. One hotel had even opened their lobby as a shelter, and the space was filled shoulder to shoulder with families.

I got in line at a pay phone and called every hotel in the area. They were either completely sold out, or they were not accessible due to roadblocks set up during the storm. I left the phone to break the bad

114

news to my bride. Someone passing by noticed the look of dejection on my face and offered directions to a place on the edge of town.

Linda wasn't excited to get back in the car, but I told her we only had to drive a few miles. The blizzard conditions were still a challenge, and I could tell the road would be impassable within the hour. I turned into the driveway of the business, a restaurant/bowling alley with an attached motel, but I got stuck again. As luck would have it, the oncoming vehicle was the same tow truck that pulled us out earlier. Dave rescued us again and charged another $10. Well worth it, I thought.

Knowing we had a place to take refuge put our minds at ease. The sole employee on the premises told us they were holding a reservation for someone. Linda and I ordered some dinner and waited to see if they would show up. The family called to say they couldn't make it and were taking refuge at a firehouse. Linda and I gratefully took their reservation, so we had a room the second night of our honeymoon. Another family arrived soon after we got our room, and they ended up sleeping on the floor of the bowling alley. We found out later the place had 30 empty rooms, but they weren't clean. Given the choice of sleeping on the floor or a dirty room, I think they would have taken the room.

The strong wind blew directly at our motel door, so I fashioned a curtain out of an extra blanket to block the draft. In the morning, the makeshift curtain was full of snow, but the storm was over. We couldn't go anywhere because of the twenty-foot drifts in some areas of the state. The clerk was still the only person running the place, and she wouldn't leave her post to take a break. Any time we saw her, she was at the counter, sometimes with her head down sleeping.

On the third day, snowplows came to clear the road in front of the bowling alley. Linda and I packed up the car and prepared to leave, *but the car wouldn't start. When I opened up the rear engine compartment, the space inside was packed with hardened snow. Even after I removed the snow, the car wouldn't start. I called AAA, and an hour later, Dave pulled up in his tow truck. He remembered us and refunded the $20 we had paid him as I signed the AAA service verification for all three saves.*

The rest of our trip was routine until we came upon a roadblock set up to keep people from entering the area we were leaving. The police had to move the barriers so we could get on the legal side of the roadblock.

By the time we arrived in New York City, we had recovered from our ordeal and we were in tourist mode. We found a USO lounge just off Times Square. Inside we found a rack of free theater tickets for active duty GIs. We took the last two tickets to the afternoon's taping of the Tonight Show with Johnny Carson. My folks lived in California and were not able to attend the wedding, so I thought this would be a great opportunity for them to see Linda as the camera panned over the audience. We called my parents to tell them to watch. Next we called Linda's parents, remembering what they said about not calling for any reason. Perhaps this was a good enough excuse to break the rules. The response from my mother-in-law was a shock, but one I never forgot.

In the meantime, Bob and I were watching television to stay updated on the storm. The snow kept falling driven by 60-mile-per-hour winds. The blizzard lasted three days. At the end of it, the news reported 103 inches of snow had fallen and we were in a state of emergency.

Monday and Tuesday came with no call from Linda and Jack. We heard one report of a couple found frozen in their car. *Oh my gosh! What if that's them?* I wondered.

Finally on the fourth day, the phone rang. "Hi Mom. Hi Dad!" came Linda's cheery voice. "We're going to be on the Johnny Carson Show."

"Linda! Do you know how worried we were? I hope your kids do this to you some day! Why didn't you call?" I scolded.

"Well you told us not to call you."

Later we heard the whole story of Jack and Linda's snowy ordeal. They learned how important it is to call your family during an emergency, even if it is during your honeymoon.

The Zillig family together on Jack and Linda's twenty-fifth wedding anniversary, 1991.

Twenty-Five Years
and Counting

Our second child was out of the nest, and the Jiffy-tite business was growing. I worked alongside Bob in the business while caring for our family, too.

Bonnie and Laird were living in the Buffalo area while he attended medical school. Susan, baby number two, arrived in 1965. Bonnie was busy caring for her family.

One day in 1967 she got a call from the woman who had choreographed the water ballet in her high school days. She wanted to recruit Bonnie for a cheerleading squad she was heading up. The Buffalo Jills cheerleaders had to be married women, and their uniforms were nothing like the NFL cheerleaders wear today. With Bonnie's background in gymnastics and water ballet, she was a natural. Bonnie

Bonnie, front row, left.

118

cheered for the squad for about a year until she and Laird moved to Key West.

In the late sixties America was in a race to the moon "before this decade [was] out" as the late President Kennedy had said. Thousands of young men were sent to fight in Vietnam while thousands more Americans protested our involvement there. Civil rights issues were growing to a fever pitch sparking riots in various cities. It was a time of innovation, but also of great crisis for our country.

On the morning of June 5, 1968, our housekeeper arrived with shocking news. Five years after the assassination of President Kennedy, his brother, Bobby was gunned down. Senator Kennedy was leaving the Ambassador Hotel in Los Angeles on his way to a press conference after winning the California Primary. Bob and I listened in disbelief as our housekeeper told us the details she had heard on the morning news. The day would soon bring news of a personal crisis.

Bob and I were getting ready for a business meeting when the phone rang again. Our housekeeper answered and quickly handed it off to Bob. I heard his half of the conversation.

"Were both men killed?" Bob asked. In that moment I knew something terrible must have happened. When Bob hung up, he explained my father and another man had been in an accident, and both had been electrocuted.

By the time the authorities called us, Mother had been sedated, so I couldn't talk to her. We heard the details of the accident later.

My parents had always dreamed of retiring in Florida, and they had lived in Fort Lauderdale for eighteen months.

They were making plans to go on a camping trip, and my father was out in the garage gathering up supplies.

Their neighbors were having a well drilled, and the day before as they were setting up, Dad offered his assistance. The boss said, "Please don't. I'm only insured for employees to handle the equipment."

The next day the man operating the drill was having trouble getting it into position. Despite the earlier warning, Dad went over to see if he could help. There had been a bad storm the night before. Just as they were moving the drilling equipment, a 7,000-volt power line came in contact with it sending a fatal jolt of electricity through my father and the man he was helping.

The neighbor across the street saw it happen and came running over. He went into the house to keep my mother away from the scene. "Don't go out there," he warned. "A wire has come down."

"Where's my husband?" she asked. "Where's Clarence?"

As soon as Bob hung up the phone, we made reservations to fly to Miami and meet my brother, Vern and his wife, Marlene. It's strange how your brain deals with things when you're going through a tragedy. As we flew to Florida, the airlines were having a contest. Each passenger had a card with a number from 1-60, representing the time we thought the airplane would fly across the Florida border. I picked the card with 58 on it and won the free car rental they were giving away. Why I would even care to pick a number I don't know, but I still remember it vividly. We needed to rent a car to drive from Miami to Ft. Lauderdale, so winning their contest was a small gift along the way.

Vernon and I made the funeral arrangements, and we went through Dad's things so Mother wouldn't have to do it. Bob and I took her with us back to our home in Olcott, New York where she stayed for the summer.

My father, Clarence Henry

One thing that comforted me was Dad didn't fear death. He had a near-death experience years earlier when he was the town supervisor of Deerfield. They were at a community picnic, and Dad had just finished running a three-legged race. Afterwards Dad sat down, turned ashen gray, and his head fell forward. A nurse in the crowd gave him some nitro-glycerin. The doctor told him he

Dad and Mother

Bonnie, David and Robin, Easter 1968, the last picture taken of Dad.

had some kind of spasm, but he would be all right. Dad later told me, "If that's what death is like, it is beautiful."

Months following Dad's accident, the insurance company settled with both families. The young drill operator who was killed in the accident had four children and a fifth one on the way. Their family rightly received hundreds of thousands of dollars in the settlement with the electric company.

My father, on the other hand, was about to turn 68 when he died, so his age was a major factor in the payment my mother received. They paid her a mere $17,000 because his earning years were over. To reduce my father's life to such an amount was tragic. His true value as a husband, father, and grandfather was priceless, no matter what his age.

Bob and I were to celebrate our 25th Wedding Anniversary just a few months after my father's death. I didn't think I could go through with the party plans, but my mother persuaded me otherwise. "Your father would want you to celebrate," she told me. Following the party in September, Mother went back to Ft. Lauderdale. Bob and I carried on with our lives, but I was still quite affected by the sudden loss of my dad. At times it put a strain on our marriage, but Bob was a very understanding man.

I was glad to see 1968 come to a close. It had been a traumatic year for me. I had no idea the new year would bring its own challenges.

In January of 1969, Bob and I went to New York City for the International Boat Show. While we were there, he complained of indigestion. It turned out to be a heart attack, and he spent a week in the hospital in New York City before they could transport him to Buffalo. He rode in an ambulance that had been a Cadillac hearse. The New York throughway was solid ice. Bob said if he survived that trip, he could survive anything.

I asked my mother to come and help me take care of Bob. We put a bed in the living room so Bob wouldn't have to climb stairs. He was there two weeks, and his doctor said Bob had to go to the hospital or he wouldn't keep him as a patient.

Bob was fifty years old and had never been hospitalized. I couldn't believe how pathetic he was. He would say things like, "Don't they know the telephone is on the wrong side of the bed?" or "Honey, would you leave me some money so I can buy a newspaper?" He complained about one thing after another.

He wouldn't let the nurses touch him, so every day I would bathe him, put on clean pajamas, and change his socks. After two weeks in the hospital, they sent him home with a strict diet. He grumbled about the restrictions. "I have to give up everything I love. They better not tell me I can't have my wife's kisses."

While Bob recovered, I ran the business. We had always worked together, and I could talk to the engineers as well as Bob did. Our parts suppliers worked well with me. In the months following Bob's heart attack, the Jiffy-tite business actually improved. I knew I could handle things in Bob's absence, but I was happy to have him back at the helm as soon as he was able.

A Shark and A Shawl

When Bonnie's husband, Laird finished medical school, they moved to Key West where he did his residency. They had met Dr. Elizabeth Olmstead, an ophthalmologist who told Laird if he specialized in her field, he would be guaranteed a position.

Bonnie and Laird settled on Sigsbee Island, the Naval base in Key West. In the two years they lived there, I visited eight times.

By the time Bonnie and Laird moved to Florida, they had two children. Money was tight for the family and Laird only got a paycheck every two weeks. They adopted an interesting tradition. On payday Laird would cash his check in $1 bills. He and Bonnie would throw the money up in the air and celebrate with a meal of hot dogs and cheap champagne.

A lot of the doctors doing their residency in Key West had docks, and they often chose funny names for their boats. One Ob/Gyn resident named his boat *Miss Conception*.

One day we took Laird's sailboat out to go snorkeling. I wanted to try scuba diving, so Laird put his air tank on me while he used his snorkel. I swam around looking at the tropical fish until I saw a big gray thing. Thinking it was a shark, I grabbed Laird and practically drowned him. When we both managed to surface, I realized the gray thing was the hull of the boat.

"I didn't know where I was, and I thought I saw a shark!" I sputtered.

Bonnie answered, "I knew right where you were. Your rear end was sticking up out of the water the whole time." That was the end of my scuba diving for many years.

On another trip to the Keys, Bonnie was participating in a fundraiser for the Old Island Restoration Foundation. It was a historic home show, and the ladies of the Officer's Wives' Club were volunteering their help. Bonnie asked if I would help out during Old Island Days by being a hostess, and I agreed.

Right after I arrived, Bonnie took me to one of the homes on the tour and gave me a red shawl to wear. The shawls were worn in remembrance of the Key West ladies who made shawls from some red merino wool cloth salvaged by some wreckers in the 1860s. One hundred years later, the restoration foundation adopted the red shawl as its signature costume for their volunteers. The long, navy blue skirt and white blouse I wore that day fit in well with their patriotic color scheme. My knee-high boots didn't hurt the look either.

One of the women told me what to say about the room in the old house. I enjoyed telling my story as each guest walked through my area. Throughout my talk, I added, "In the olden days," as I explained how people lived in the Keys during the 1800s. When my shift was almost over, a lady came to relieve me. She listened as I gave my spiel. I must have been a convincing storyteller, because she asked me, "How long have you lived here?"

"I just got here two hours ago," I answered.

After two years, Laird's tour of duty was up. My last night there was very emotional. I took a bike ride by myself all around Sigsbee Island. Tears streamed down my face because I loved the island paradise so much and knew I would never have another visit.

The next February, Cece, the wife of the Naval Commander in Key West, called me. She was in charge of the fundraiser. "Are you coming down to the Keys?" she asked. "I'm depending on you to help out with the home tour again." I had no reason to visit since Bonnie didn't live there any more, but I was flattered that Cece wanted me back.

For a Few Dollars More

I fell in love with a man in 1943 who loved sailing, but Bob laid aside that passion so he could raise a family. Early in our marriage we sold the eighteen-foot boat he built in his parents' garage when he was a teenager. With the responsibility of six mouths to feed, there was never enough extra money to buy another boat. Bob didn't give up on that dream, but it was twenty years before he saw it realized.

Maybe I should clarify that. His next boat wasn't much more than a large toy. He bought a nine-foot, Styrofoam dinghy for about $100 at a department store. It looked like a glorified ice chest. We would tie it to the roof of the car whenever we took the family out for a weekend. The kids and I would swim while Bob sailed, or should I say bobbed around, in the one-man ice chest. Since it was so small, we went boating in the Finger Lakes region of New York.

I'm sure while sailing in the dinghy Bob imagined himself the captain of a beautiful sailboat. We eventually gave the dinghy to a cousin and Bob went looking for something bigger.

We bought a nineteen-foot sailboat called the Mariner. Bob must have felt like Christopher Columbus as he set sail on the twenty-mile journey from the Niagara River to Olcott. All he had for directions was a road map, which didn't do him much good on the water.

I was in the car with the children and planned to meet him in Olcott. About halfway there I went down a road to a farmhouse not far from the lake. The wind was out of the east and had picked up, so I knew he would have to tack. That meant sailing at a forty-five degree angle into the wind and then zig zagging until he got to his destination. I couldn't see Bob, so I went on to Olcott.

When I arrived at the clubhouse, someone asked, "Is your name Shirley? Your husband has been trying to reach you." Bob had turned back to the Niagara River because he knew he wouldn't be able to make it in those winds.

Several days later we made another attempt, this time with me onboard. Bonnie took our car with the kids to meet us in Olcott. Sailing together was such an adventure for us. We had never sailed from one point to another. Bob taught me the sailor's terminology so I could understand his directions.

Our delight was short lived as we spent our first night on the boat tied up at the dock. We had a boom tent that went over the boom and tied to both sides of the boat. Bob slept on one side and I slept on the other. All night long we were thrown back and forth as the boat bobbed on our lines at the dock. We didn't get any sleep. That's when we decided we needed a bigger boat.

Bob used to tell a story about a man who wanted to buy a boat. It went something like this:

> This guy goes out to get a rowboat. "I need a rowboat," he tells the salesman.
>
> "I can fix you right up," he replies. "But for a few dollars more, I can give you a motor for it."

"Okay," the guy says. "That sounds like a good idea."

"Sure is," says the salesman. "But for a few dollars more, I can sell you a boat with a little cabin on it. Then if it rains or gets cold, you're all set."

"Okay."

"As long as you're looking at a boat with a cabin, you should know that for a few dollars more, you can move up to a cabin with a sleeping area."

"I never thought of that," says the guy.

"And since you're going to be sleeping on the boat, you'll need one with a galley. You can get one for a few dollars more," the salesman added.

"That makes sense," the guy says.

"If you're spending so much time on your boat, you'll want one with a head. For a few dollars more you can add a shower."

"Sounds like a good idea to me," says the guy.

On and on the story goes. We could definitely identify with the guy in that story. Bob *was* the guy in the story!

After only one season with our nineteen-footer, we were on our way to a boat dealership in Rochester, sixty miles away. All the way there Bob kept telling me, "I'm going to be a tough nut to crack. I'm not taking their first price. I'm going to dicker him down."

"Yes, honey," I said.

As soon as we pulled into the boat dealer's lot and saw the beautiful Coronado 25, Bob exclaimed, "I'll take it! I'll take it!"

The salesman didn't do any nut cracking that day. They delivered our new boat to Olcott and we christened it the Carousel. We sailed around Olcott a lot with her and had a lot of fun.

Bob at the helm of a trimaran

Olcott Beach was a big tourist attraction in the early 1900s. Even Teddy Roosevelt visited the area in 1899. Following his visit, a trolley line was built from Lockport to Olcott Beach. With accessible transportation, more people came and needed lodging. Several hotels were built, the largest being the Olcott Beach Hotel. It was situated on the sandy lakeshore and had its own amusement rides. In Olcott's heyday, the trolleys brought more than 100,000 tourists every year.

The Great Depression of the 1930s impacted Olcott Beach's tourism industry. People didn't have the money to spend days at a resort. In addition, they could drive their cars to the beach and go home the same day. The trolley and hotel became obsolete, and in 1937 the hotel was torn down. In the 1940s, many of the big bands played in the outdoor amphitheater.

When we bought our cottage at Olcott, the amusement parks were no longer in operation. Boaters still enjoyed the area, but gone were the resort hotels and big amusement parks. In recent years there has been a drive to restore the old-time amusement parks of Olcott Beach.

We joined the Olcott Yacht Club when we started sailing regularly. People said I didn't look old enough to have four kids. I responded with, "Oh the kids are from Bob's *first* marriage." It was a running gag we joked about for years.

On one forty-mile trip to Toronto with the kids we sailed at night while they slept. We had two berths on either side of the boat and two small berths under the cockpit. It was a miserable, rainy night, and Bob and I were exhausted when we pulled up to the pier at about 11:00 that night. We got through customs and found a yacht club where we could tie up for the night. Bob and I turned in, but the kids were up and raring to go. It took awhile to get them settled down once again, and we all went to sleep.

The next morning I looked out one of our little portholes to see nothing but white. It looked like somebody had covered the porthole with paper. A thick fog had settled over the lake, and we would have to wait for it to lift. We had no other mode of transportation and nothing to do.

We had been anxious to get out in the boat that spring, but we hadn't taken into account this natural occurrence. Warm air over the colder water caused the dense fog, and it certainly put a damper on our little outing. The sun burned off the fog and we made the return trip. Being jammed into the cabin of our boat for hours made us realize we needed a bigger boat.

A houseboat seemed like a good solution for our family, so in 1968. we got a forty-three-foot Nautiline with a redesigned interior. Bob wanted to name it Passing Wind, but we settled on Passing Fancy. There were about twelve boats in this one area of Olcott Beach where we kept the houseboat.

There was a big sailboat in the slip next to us. Previously owned by Ted Turner, the American Eagle, as she was called, had been a contender for the America's Cup Race. Turner sold the custom-built sailboat because it hadn't done well as a racer. The current owners, Herb and Jerry, owned a chain of Cadet Cleaners in Canada. They chose to keep the boat at Olcott to avoid paying duty on it in Canada. Herb and Jerry spent many weekends on the boat, and we became good friends. Herb used to read his paper on deck, wad it up, and toss it onto our boat when he was done.

Bob and I, Steven and Chrissie on our houseboat.

Herb and Jerry invited us to their daughter's wedding in Toronto. We took the houseboat across the lake with two other couples riding with us. It was a lavish affair, so we brought our formals and furs. The taxi we called waited for us at the dock. Bob and the other guys let the women off and went to park the boat. As we got into the taxi, I saw an opportunity for some fun. I called out, "We had a great weekend, fellas. Thanks for the furs. Call us again when you're in town."

My friends, Chris and Jeanie, picked up on my joke as we rode in the back of the taxi. "How shall we register? Smith, Young, and Brown again?" Jeanie asked.

The poor cab driver kept looking at us in the rearview mirror. He was probably happy to let us off at the hotel where seven limousines waited to take the guests to the wedding.

We made that crossing to Toronto so many times over the years. We usually had a contest with everyone on board. Whoever spotted land first got a dime from the captain. As time went on and the kids grew up, the amount went up to a quarter. On one of our trips, the captain shelled out much more than a quarter. We were by ourselves, probably for an anniversary weekend. While shopping in Toronto, I walked by a jacket in the fur department of Eaton's on my way to the ladies' room. "Oh, look at this," I said, admiring the brown and white mink pattern and the white fox trim.

"Why don't you try it on?" Bob suggested.

"Okay," I said. I caressed the soft fur as I looked at myself in the mirror. Then I took it off and hung it back on the hanger.

"I like it," Bob said. "I want to buy it for you."

"Why do I need a fur coat? We live in Florida." I put the jacket back on the rack. "I'm going to the restroom," I said.

We finished our shopping and went back to the boat later that day. I laid awake

134

arguing with myself. *Shirley, are you crazy? Your husband wants to buy you a mink coat! Why don't you let him?*

The next morning, I told Bob I wanted to go back to the store and buy the coat. After that I was not so quick to turn down a gift from my husband.

* * *

On windy days, Olcott harbor was very rough. The design of the piers preserved every wave as it came into the harbor. There were many nights we drove home in our pajamas because we couldn't sleep with the boat rocking. That's when we decided we needed a house. We found a cottage overlooking the harbor and started negotiating on it in July of 1969, the same week as the first moon landing.

The house dated back over 100 years. It had served as rowboat storage at one time, and later as a restaurant. It had a rich history, but it was in serious need of a facelift.

We hired a contractor to do the remodel. He pulled down the old knotty-pine paneling and replaced the door to the porch overlooking the harbor. Because of its age, the structure leaned toward the water. The contractor had to shore up the walls eight inches in order to install the sliding glass doors.

The cottage at Olcott

The cottage had a huge basement, but three-fourths of it was actually above ground. It was almost like living in a three-story house because of it. The lower level had huge picture windows. With three bedrooms, a large living room and dining room, and a small kitchen, our summer cottage housed the family comfortably.

The cottage became part of a commercial after the lower level flooded one spring. Our son-in-law's brother called us. "I just heard there's a storm in Olcott," he reported. "They're sandbagging a house, and I think it's yours."

We immediately went to check on the situation. The police stopped us at a barricade, but when we explained it was our house, they let us through. Water had broken through the basement level, and the fire department was there sandbagging to save the house.

Later an insurance company used the news footage of water coming into our house as the voice over said, "Make sure your home is protected."

The cottage made it through that storm and many years later, it's still in our family.

True to Bob's boat story, we went bigger and better on our next boat. We went back to the dealer in Rochester where we saw a gorgeous thirty-five-foot sailboat. We talked to the people that owned it and found out there was a sister ship just like it for sale. It had been dismasted when the wind knocked the mast over during a race. The mast wasn't supported down through the hull, so it couldn't take it when the winds came up.

The entire boat was refurbished at the factory. They put a large, stainless-steel hole down through the cabin to secure the mast. In essence we were getting a brand new boat at half price.

The Bounty, as we called her, was delivered up in Clayton, New York where the St. Lawrence River joins Lake Ontario. We had some neighbors take us up there, and we were going to sail it back with Chris and Steven. Our friends stayed with us as we bought supplies and got settled in, then they drove our car home.

The first night we went to Main Duck Island, forty or fifty miles into the Lake from the river. We had a chart and we saw a cove we could go into. I had an interesting way of navigating. I had a trivet with asbestos on one side and metal on the other. I used that as my straight edge as I drew a line from the compass rose on the chart to our destination. I navigated from point A to point B, and then moved the compass rose and my trivet and drew another line. With my ingenuity and my trivet, we sailed right to our destination.

It was April but still very cold on our trip. The next morning the deck was covered with a thin sheet of ice. Bob had to crawl out on his hands and knees to raise the anchor.

We had used a little heater inside the cabin all night. I didn't realize it was an alcohol heater, and the next morning Steven was sick from inhaling the fumes. We got him out on deck so he could breathe the clean air, and we soon got rid of that heater.

We had to motor the whole ninety miles to Rochester. It was a clear day, but there was no wind. When we pulled into a dock to get some fuel it started snowing. I held my hands around the fuel tank to make sure we wouldn't get any water into it.

Steven and Chrissie with Bounty on one of our trips to Toronto

We spent the night there and continued on the sixty miles to Olcott the next morning.

We enjoyed the Bounty for awhile, but it was a leaky boat. We attributed it to the refurbishing job. I soon tired of catching water with pans all the time, so we sold it.

Our next boat was a forty-one-foot Morgan Out Islander. It was a beauty to look at but a dog to sail. Because of its size, it should have had a longer keel to give it some stability. Instead it had a little skag, like a shark's fin. Any time we wanted to come about, we had to put the motor on or we couldn't turn well.

The galley was a problem too. It was so wide I needed tongs to reach into the cupboard. The icebox was deep enough for a person to sit in. I had to bend way over to get things out of it. We learned that a sailboat has to be more than beautiful to be enjoyed.

Me wearing a t-shirt matching Lola's face.

We continued to trade in boats to upgrade or try something new. One time we purchased a catamaran, and Bob wanted to name it The Banana Split. We had a couple boats we named Lola, because whatever Lola wants, Lola gets. We painted a face on the stern of one of our Lola's and gave her long, wispy eyelashes.

One of our boats, a Shucker, was featured on the cover of a sailing magazine. We loved sailing, but we owned several motorized

138

boats over the years too. For a few dollars more, we bought a 53-foot Hatteras yacht, the biggest in the Zillig fleet. It was a long way from Bob's styrofoam sailboat to the yacht, and we made many wonderful memories sailing together.

The Shucker we had built
in Cape Coral

Our 53-foot Hatteras

Blue Skies and Movie Stars

One of our more memorable sailing trips was from Norfolk, Virginia to Olcott, New York on our boat, the Blue Skies II. We set out one Sunday afternoon in June of 1973. We planned to travel from the Chesapeake Bay at Norfolk, up the east coast, and through New York's inland waterways to Olcott. I had laid out the entire course with time, speed, and distance on charts on my living room floor. Our friends, Ron and Virginia and Nikki and Jules, or Julie as we called him, came along. We were all anxious to start our adventure.

In spite of our enthusiasm, the gray skies that day proved to be a sign of things to come. First we had some trouble with our compass headings, but we resolved that by setting course with the sea buoys. The real problems started around 11:00 the first night out. We heard a hissing noise and smoke poured out of the engine room. The engine died and we sat drifting. Bob tried sailing while looking for the trouble, but there was no wind and he had no idea what happened. Reluctantly at 1:00 a.m. he called the Coast Guard for assistance.

Between drifting and fog closing in, the Coast Guard didn't reach us until 5:00 a.m. We were all cold and tired. They towed us in to Chincoteague Inlet where we anchored around 9:00 that morning.

We found out the hissing was the pressure relief valve on the hot water tank. We thought we had drained the air from all the sink faucets, but we missed one. The air in the lines built up and popped the release valve, as it was designed to do, spraying the engine with water. Once it was dried out, we were good to go. The Coast Guard requested that we stay in contact and report our position along the way. We did that and arrived at the Ocean City Harbor around 7:00 Monday night. The Coast Guard sent a boat out to meet us, but we ran aground coming into the harbor. Bob stayed at the wheel while the other five of us rocked the boat by running side to side on the deck. The people on shore watched and laughed, and we laughed along with them. Our rocking the boat worked, and we were free.

We tied up at a gas dock for the night. Even so, I was thankful for a chance to take a shower and get a good night's sleep.

The next morning, we had a leisurely breakfast and set sail for Atlantic City. We made our marks on time all day until heavy fog closed in like cotton batten. We had to call the Coast Guard again for assistance, and it took them a half hour to find us. The fog lifted like a curtain as we approached the harbor.

Coast Guard regulations require three means to signal in an emergency: a signal bell, an air horn, and a whistle. We had not taken the time to mount the bell on the bulkhead. When the Coast Guard showed up to lead us into the harbor, they gave us a citation for not having the bell mounted.

Before leaving the dock on Wednesday under gray skies, I gave Bob the coordinates to the first buoy. Bob made a comment, "It's so nice. Why should we even go there? Let's shorten the route."

Almost as soon as he said how beautiful it was, fog enveloped us. I had to scramble to get us back on course. We used the depth finder to help us locate our position.

Fog came and went as clouds threatened rain all day. We made about eight miles per hour. Traveling from the lower New York Harbor past Ellis Island offered a beautiful sight of the Statue of Liberty. I choked up as I thought about the millions of immigrants who saw the same sight as they entered the harbor.

Bob was proud we made it all the way to New York in one piece without further assistance from the Coast Guard. I wrote in the log, "I hope they don't miss us too much."

We found our dock at a marina, but it was a crummy place with no facilities. We did have a little excitement though. The place was swarming with policemen until two drug addicts on the boat next to us were arrested and taken away.

As we left the dock in drizzling rain our fourth day out, it looked like our wonderful trip was going down the drain. We were all a bit cranky.

The weather cleared and we made about 75 miles up the Hudson River to Kingston. Nikki studied the pilot book and was rattling off nautical terms. Her favorite one was snatch-block, an apparatus used to hold the sail lines where you want them.

We stopped for gas just short of Kingston, hoping to get supplies at the marina, but when we arrived, we found out the groceries and laundromat were two miles away. We called a cab, but had to wait so long for it we decided to borrow a pick-up truck from the marina. I shopped while my friends Julie and Nikki did laundry.

We decided the whole trip should be made into a movie with a cast of thousands. As we saw people along the way, we cast them as celebrity look alikes. It gave us a distraction from the delays of the trip, but Bob didn't like our little game. He would shush us and say, "You shouldn't talk so loud. They'll hear you." He took his Captain responsibilities seriously, as he should. He did have a lot on his shoulders. Because of his reprimands, we nicknamed him Captain Nice, and the name stuck with him.

Captain Nice

We turned in early so we could leave at 5:00 a.m. the next morning. We wanted to arrive at the next stop by 4:00 p.m. so we could get someone to unstep the mast. This involves taking the mast down, laying it on the boat and securing each end on cross pieces on deck. We had to do this because some of the bridges don't open on the Erie Canal.

We ate breakfast once we were underway, and I wondered what crisis awaited us. We didn't have long to wait. Heavy rainstorms hit us with little visibility. The channels were narrow, and there were a lot of tugboats to dodge. It rained for ten hours or more. I plotted our course and gave Bob the compass headings because we couldn't see to navigate. Everybody was getting punchy.

We made good time to Albany until we arrived at the first swing bridge. It was broken and would have to be opened by five or six men hand cranking it. The man called out, "The bridge is broken. It will be about an hour and a half to get it open. Do you want to wait?" What a question! What else could we do, go back out to the ocean? We thought it was a good time to have a drink, and it did help pass the time. Finally the men came, did their job, and we passed through.

As we approached Troy, I tried unsuccessfully to raise the marine telephone operator to call the boat yard. Lock one was ready for traffic when we got there, so we followed three other boats through with no trouble. We cast the workman in our make-believe movie as *Rodney Dangerfield* and his dog as *Rin Tin Tin*. *Andy Griffin* tossed us the line and lo and behold, *Peter Lorre* was the captain of one of the other boats in the lock.

We went through a few more bridges with ease, but the last one was broken. We couldn't believe we had to wait another hour and a half for repairs. We called ahead to Matlon's Marina to tell them we would be late, so they arranged to have someone come in to unstep our mast. We ate dinner anchored in the Hudson River while waiting for the repair. We finally made it through that bridge and on to the shipyard.

The workman and his son arrived at Matlon's around 6:30. The rain came down in buckets as we unstepped the mast. While Nikki held one end of it she complained, "I can't swat the mosquitos and the rain is running down my arms into my bra. I'm soaking wet!"

It took about three and a half hours to do the job. Between the pouring rain and the hungry mosquitoes, we desperately needed another celebration. We decided to spend the night across the river at the Troy Yacht Club where *Marjorie Main* gave us a warm welcome. When Julie saw her, he asked, "Do you have showers? Hot water?" She replied yes to both questions, and he jumped off the boat and gave her a big hug.

Sitting inside the club, we found *Jean Stapleton* and *Keenan Wynn* who were very accommodating. They gave us a tour of their club and even gave us mats for our feet in the showers.

It was by far the wettest and funniest day of the trip. After our celebration, we all took delicious showers and retired our weary bodies for the night.

It was a good thing we took refreshment when we had the chance. The next day was intense as we started our journey through the many locks on the Erie Canal.

We went through the first seven locks with ease, but lock eight was another story. As we approached it, the gates were open causing turbulence in the

Going through locks on one of our trips.

waters. It took some skillful maneuvering by our captain to get us into the lock.

Approaching the next lock, we experienced more rushing water like a whirlpool, and it almost swung our stern into the iron walls of the lock. Not only that, Bob had to dodge some large logs in the process. Heavy snow in the New England area had melted and brought logs into the waterway. Conquering that lock called for another celebration and lunch.

Lock number eleven was another hairy experience, but by then we were feeling like pros. We didn't see many boats along the way, but we met a man we cast as *Lionel Barrymore* in lock eleven. He told us he rode the trolley cars in the early days of Olcott.

We breezed through lock thirteen and met a *Wally Cox* look alike. We used his phone to call our friend, Mary and asked her to buy a few groceries and bring them to our rendezvous spot.

The next day was Sunday, and we had been on our trip a full week. With all our troubles it seemed longer, but at least we had great company with our friends along.

We continued on through the locks with no trouble until lock seventeen. They had no power causing an hour delay. While we waited, we picked wild strawberries and flowers on the banks.

We met up with Mary and her family and gave them a tour of the boat. Our pantry was stocked once again with the supplies Mary brought to us. On lock twenty-two we stopped for water and gas, but the place was rundown. We realized later we got some bad water there. We were tired and discouraged from all the delays.

The next phase of our trip involved getting across Oneida Lake. Its shallow depth causes the water to rile up fast if the weather gets rough. With our mast strapped down on deck, any bouncing around would be a disaster. We gave a collective sigh of relief when we made it across the lake to Brewerton without incident. We did have an issue finding our marina though. The lighting navigation system left much to be desired. The lighted buoys were set so far apart, we couldn't see well enough to find our dock. We went aground when we tried to pull into a place we thought was our marina. Once we got directions, we found the right place and tied up in a lovely spot for the night.

The next stretch of water showed us some beautiful homes. As we passed a bridge, we approached the home of my Aunt Loretta and Uncle Bob Gang. They were expecting us, and tooted an air horn as we passed their dock. They drove over to Fulton where we met later for a short visit.

The trip through the locks that day went very quickly, and we pulled into Oswego Marina at noon sharp. We gassed up and cleaned out our water. The sun beat down on us and there was no air moving. We pulled over to the mast-stepping dock, had lunch and waited. It only took 45 minutes to step the mast. The man really knew what he was doing. We took a break in an air-conditioned lounge before continuing on Lake Ontario to Little Sodus Bay. We tied up at the hotel at 7:30 p.m., and it was so hot we dangled our feet in the water while we had a martini celebration. We met *Van Heflin* and his family from England.

We were up at 7:00 the next morning and enjoyed a quiet breakfast dockside. We pulled away, motored out, and hoisted the main before the entrance piers. We started sailing, but with the puffy air we didn't need the jib. We furled it and continued sailing and motoring. We made about eight miles per hour with Otto, the auto pilot at the helm. We used Otto a lot on the trip. It is a contraption with extending arms which lay across the cockpit seats. The Captain puts in a heading and attaches the tiller to the auto pilot. One time we had to send Otto, the auto, back to California to be serviced. We wrote a note for the technician,

"Otto needs open heart surgery. Please don't take too long because we've forgotten how to steer."

We arrived at the Rochester Yacht Club in the afternoon. It sure seemed funny to sit around at such an early hour. We took showers and celebrated at the Rochester Port. We went to dinner at the Harbor Inn Restaurant and even had a few dances. It was a fitting way to commemorate the final night of our adventure.

The morning of July 4th we rose at 5:30 a.m. and pulled away at 6:00 a.m. sharp. We wanted to be in Olcott in time for the annual Sail Past, a celebration for the incoming Commodore of the Yacht Club. The boats line up to give a respectful salute by dipping their ensigns or flags as they pass and each Captain salutes.

Lake Ontario looked like a mirror with no air for sailing when we started out. We ate breakfast underway and got together to scrub the boat using lake water and 409. What a difference that made. After her long, dirty trip, Blue Skies II was presentable for her arrival in homeport.

We enjoyed our wonderful trip and the company of friends. We learned a lot, but the top prize went to Salty Nikki who corrected everyone with her nautical knowledge gained en route.

Many of our friends from the yacht club gave us a horn salute as we entered Olcott's harbor, and we made it in time for the Sail Past.

As we neared our cottage, we saw a white sheet hanging from the porch balcony. Bonnie and Laird made a sign, "This is it! Olcott Welcomes Blue Skies." It was great to be home.

We all agreed we would do it again in spite of the troubles, all of us that is, except Captain Nice. Bob was glad to hang up his captain's hat, put his feet up and rest awhile.

Raising a Successor

It's cliché to expect your son to take over the family business one day. We dreamed about it, but never forced it on Steven. We enjoyed watching our only son grow into manhood.

When Steven was about nine years old, he wanted a mini-bike. He had saved up about $500 and we offered him a business loan from Jiffy-tite for the rest. He paid us $5 a week, and I showed him how to figure the compound interest. Every week he wrote his payments in a spiral notebook. It broke our hearts to take that money from him, but he learned a valuable lesson from it.

Even before that first mini-bike, Steven's mechanical skills were evident. Bob and I were both mechanically inclined, so it wasn't surprising that Steven was too. His friends would bring their bikes or motorcycles over, and he tinkered with them. Bob's tools always ended up in the driveway. "Now I know how my father felt when I did that," Bob would say as he surveyed the scene.

Steven had a nice group of friends growing up, but they were always doing something funny. One day I came home and they were rolling peanuts across the floor with their noses. Another time they cooked slices of bologna on our indoor grill. I learned to expect the unexpected.

We did a lot of sailing with the family, and we often took Steven's friends with us. It was a challenge to keep enough food on board for them. I stocked up the boat for a weekend trip to Toronto once, and as soon as we left the dock, the boys were down in the galley eating. By the time we got to the other side of the lake six hours later, we had to buy more groceries.

During the seventies, streaking, running naked in public, became a popular fad for young people. Steven wasn't one to enjoy ceremony, and one day he had a short streak of rebellion. Wearing nothing but a ski mask, he ran across the stage in front of a full school auditorium. He made it to his friend's get-away car, and I didn't hear about it until much later. Steven pulled some silly pranks, but he wasn't into the drug scene like so many teens.

We were proud of all four of our kids, and it was exciting to see each one of them graduate from high school. When it was Steven's turn, he chose a two-year college in Williamsville, New York before transferring to Cornell University. That November he called to ask me how to make the green bean casserole I serve for Thanksgiving dinner.

"How many cans of green beans do you use, Mom? He asked.

"That depends on how many people you are serving. How many?"

"Ninety," he answered.

"Ninety?"

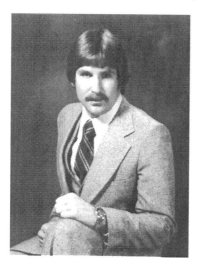

Steven Zillig, 1976

"Yes, the two floors of our dorm are getting together," he explained. Steven didn't have much cooking skill then, but he learned to love it. He had a girlfriend back then who dreamed of working in the restaurant business. She got into Cornell's cooking school with Steven's help. As their relationship became more serious, she decided to focus on her dream and they broke up. Steven recovered from the break up, but retained his love of cooking.

When Steven was in his early teens, he worked in our Jiffy-tite business packing boxes for shipment. It was a great start, but we wanted him to experience the working world before coming to work for us after college. Following his graduation, we suggested he go out and work for someone else for a year. He went to Florida where Bonnie and Laird were living and worked for the Harris Corporation for a year.

Steven believed in hard work with integrity. One time his boss asked to have something on his desk Monday morning. He worked all weekend on it so he could turn it in on time. Thursday morning it was still there, untouched. Steven learned some things about how not to treat employees from that experience.

When Steven came to work for us, Bob told our manager, Al, "Steven is our son, but you're the boss. He's just a kid learning, so whatever you say goes. I'll back you on that." We found out it was easier said than done.

We met Al years before when we were in the sports car club together. At that time anyone working for us had access to our home above the business. We felt we knew him well enough to trust him. We learned a lot of his idiosyncrasies as we worked closely for several years.

Al lived about thirty-five miles from us. When we had the normal winter snowstorms, Al didn't adjust his travel time to account for snowy roads. Getting to work twenty minutes late was on time to him.

One day he was running later than usual, and he was pulled over for speeding. He gave the officer the excuse of being late for work, and the man let him off with a warning. A short time later, the officer stopped at a diner. There sat Al having his morning coffee. "I thought you were late for work," said the officer.

I don't know if the cop gave him a ticket, but the crazy thing was Al told us the whole story later. In some ways, Al didn't know how to be a friend and an employee too.

Al was very particular when boxing up parts for shipping. He lined up ten connectors in a neat row before putting them in the box. There were ten parts to a box, and ten boxes to a carton. Filling the shelves gave Al a sense of accomplishment, and he didn't seem to enjoy shipping them out. We were more interested in selling the stock than looking at full shelves.

When we hired Steven, Bob and I were living in Florida. I did all the bookkeeping from home, and Bob traveled to Buffalo about once a month to keep tabs on the business. Our absence created an awkward position for both Al and Steven. Steven knew his place as a new employee, but he also recognized ways to make operations more efficient. It was hard for him to say anything to Al who was older and had more seniority. Al was not a decision maker, so if something came up at the shop, they waited until Bob came back to resolve the issue.

We finally realized we had to do something or our business would disintegrate. We took the coward's way out and asked Steven to let Al go. We felt uncomfortable about it and never kept in touch with Al after that.

Steven did a great job with the responsibility of managing Jiffy-tite. In 1981, he married a lovely girl, Barbie. She became another daughter to me, and we were so blessed to welcome her into the family. She married into the Jiffy-tite company too, and worked alongside Steven in much the same way Bob and I did for so many years.

Steven and Barbie, 1981

Steven brought fresh ideas to the business. One adaptation of our product was for radiators. Harrison Radiators stockpiled their inventory before delivery and wanted to insure no water would get inside the radiators and rust. Steven and Bob designed a plug that sealed the radiators and broke off when they were delivered.

As time went on, Jiffy-tite became known as a problem solving company. Businesses would come to us with problems, sometimes unrelated to our connectors, and our engineers worked on the solutions.

By 1985, we were ready to permanently hand the reins of Jiffy-tite over to Steven. We stayed on a couple more years before completely retiring.

Jiffy-tite's partnership with DME took the business into the automotive industry in the eighties. The first automotive application went into a 1986 GMC pick-up truck. Steven got the first patent in 1986. We had not applied for patents previously because it's difficult to get one and even more troublesome to police it. We felt we had a better product than anyone in the industry, and that precluded our need for earlier patents.

Jiffy-tite continued to grow under Steven's leadership, and he moved the business from Clarence to a rented building in 1987. He purchased an Apple 64 computer to help manage the business.

Just like his dad, Steven looked for innovations. The first automatic assembly machine was built from spare parts and produced 6,000 parts a day.

When Bob saw the tremendous growth of the company, he told Steven, "I envisioned all of this sitting at the winding machine many years ago." Steven far surpassed our dreams for him as a successor.

Fly, Granny, Fly

My dream to fly sat dormant for decades. In 1975 I was pushing fifty and the dream remained out of reach. Every time Bob and I drove from our home in Williamsville to the cottage in Olcott, we passed a sign, "Learn to Fly: $595." I'd say, "Someday I'm going to take flying lessons."

Bob would answer, "I don't know who's going to fly with you."

He had had a bad experience as a young man when a pilot took him for a ride and he got so sick he couldn't see straight. Bob knew he would never be a pilot, and that disappointment spilled over onto my dream too. In spite of his initial comments, my candle of desire grew a little brighter every time I read that sign.

Our daughter, Bonnie, had taken up flying when she and Laird lived in Key West. Laird could fly at a tenth of the normal cost, only $2.10 an hour at the time, while he logged hours for his commercial license. Bonnie was the first woman to get her pilot's license at the Key West Naval Flying School.

When they moved up to Merritt Island, Bonnie flew from the small airport there. Once when we were visiting, Bonnie said, "Mom, I have a surprise for you. I've arranged for your first flying lesson."

It was so exhilarating to sit in the cockpit and handle the controls of an airplane after dreaming about it for so many years. The short flight with an instructor provided the nudge I needed. I signed up for flying lessons as soon as we got home.

Howard and Bea Lee owned the airport I had seen with the sign. Their son, Fred, became my flight instructor. Any time I flew with Fred, I would mentally picture myself flying alone as I prepared for my first solo flight. The student never knows when it's going to happen. I knew I could be flying around, doing touch and goes where I land and take off again, and my instructor might jump out and say, "You're on your own."

When that day came, instead of imagining myself alone in the airplane, I pretended Fred was in the plane with me. I felt so comfortable in the airplane, like I was born to fly.

My training included dealing with emergency scenarios the instructor doled out so I would be well prepared for anything that could happen. That included putting the plane in an unusual attitude while my feet and hands were off the yoke and rudders and my eyes were covered. I practiced recovering to straight and level flying within twenty seconds of taking the yoke again.

The first thing I did was check airspeed. If it is slow, it means the plane is climbing; fast means it is descending. I should stop the climb or descent and level off. Next I looked at the wings to see if they were tipped or straight and I would correct that. I also checked the altimeter. All this happened within a few seconds. No matter what my instructor did to test my skill, I recovered with a smile on my face.

Before I could get my private pilot's license, I had to log at least three hours of night flying. The night landings I did were tricky because of the drive-in theater across the road from the airport. As I did my approach, I could see the movie playing on the big screen. They were showing *Erica Goes to Hollywood* one night, a sleazy, low-budget film. It was hard to keep my mind focused as I flew past the screen. Then I had to avoid the telephone wires and a large, bushy tree in my approach to the runway.

My flight instructor and I flew many trips to Batavia, thirty miles away. The normal day included lunch there and the return trip to Lockport. I soon tired of seeing the same old things and eating from the airport diner's limited menu. *If I ever get this airplane alone, I'm going to fly far away from Batavia* I thought.

On my first solo cross country flight, I was supposed to fly to Hornell, New York. I got there and announced my position. When I landed, I slid back the cockpit cover of the airplane and grabbed my log book. "Well I made it to Hornell," I announced to the man leaning against the airport building.

"No you didn't, honey. This is Cornell," he corrected.

How could I have landed at the wrong airport? All I could think of to do was look at the new watch Bob had given me for my birthday that day. "Well, I sure did make good time!"

Like any smart woman who is lost, I stopped in at the desk and asked for directions. When I took off again, I soon realized I still didn't know my position, so I called the tower. "Could you tell me where I am?"

As part of the checklist before take off, the pilot matches the direction gyro to the compass. I had forgotten to do that, so I took off and flew in the wrong direction. I corrected my course and headed north toward Lake Ontario. I kept flying and saw a city ahead of me. *Hmm. I wonder what city that is.* When I flew closer, I realized it was BATAVIA. I started laughing and cussing out the airplane. "You don't know anything but to fly to Batavia!"

When I finally landed at my home airport in Lockport, I laughed as I told my instructor the whole story. The more I talked, the angrier he looked.

"Didn't you check your course? Didn't you look for check points?" He really bawled me out.

"Oh shut up," I snapped. "I made it back in one piece didn't I?"

One of my big motivations to get my pilot's license was to buy a plane so we could fly to Florida to see Bonnie. A few months into my  flight training, Howard and Fred flew us to Cleveland to buy our first plane, a Grumman AA5. Howard flew my plane back since I didn't have my license yet. I was more excited than a kid on Christmas morning

I started ground school and flight training in February of 1975. I was ready for my final check ride in August, but after three tries in three weeks being grounded by weather, I felt like a coiled spring ready to twang. Finally one day we had clear skies. As I did my check list before take off, something flew into the plane through the open canopy, but the examiner couldn't find it to let it out. It turned out to be a grasshopper, but we both agreed it wouldn't distract either of us, so I took off. After the flight as we were ready to leave the plane and I knew I'd passed, the grasshopper hopped up onto my lap and flew away. It wasn't until later I realized the significance of a grasshopper accompanying me.

The Grasshoppers Club, a Florida-based group of female pilots flew together once a month. When the grasshopper flew

with me that day, I felt those ladies were saying, "Well done, Shirley. We were with you all the way."

When I received my pilot's license, Fred lettered the airport sign to read, "Shirley Zillig, Private Pilot." Bob was so proud of his pilot wife. He posed for a picture by the sign with empty pants pockets hanging out. I told him I couldn't have done it without his understanding, his moral support, and his MONEY. This was just the beginning of Bob supporting my flying habit, but he was happy to do it. From then on, everybody at the airport referred to me as The Flying Grandmother. I always said, "If I can do it, anyone can."

My instructor knew Bob and I would be flying to Florida soon, so he had prepared me for any type of weather. "I want you to know how much weather you can fly through to be safe and legal," he said. "You see that weather up ahead? That's your notification. Don't fly into that."

In October, Bob and I flew our first trip to Florida to see Bonnie and Laird. The first leg of the trip ended in Jacksonville, and overnight the weather deteriorated. I was only rated for VFR (visual flight rules). The weather had grounded me. Disappointed, I picked up the phone to call Bonnie.

"I really wanted this first trip to be perfect," I told her. "I wanted to make it all the way without incident."

"You did the right thing, Mom," she responded. "You saw the weather coming in and you made a decision as the pilot in command."

Bob and I spent another night in Jacksonville, but the next day greeted us with more pouring rain. "We should sell this blankity-blank airplane!" Bob griped.

With our frustration level at its peak, we left the plane and rented a car to drive the last couple hours to Bonnie's. At the end of our visit, Halloween day to be exact, Bonnie flew us back to Jacksonville in her Cherokee 6. As we prepared to leave the airport, she told me, "When we take off, we'll go side by side on the runway, and I'll do the radio work."

The tower cleared us both for take off and called again to tell us to resume normal navigation. "By the way," the man in the tower radioed, "There's a target off your right wing about a quarter of a mile."

"I know," Bonnie answered. "It's my mother." There was not another word from the tower.

Who needs a witch's broom on Halloween when you can fly high in your own airplane?

We're Taking the Luggage!

Bonnie continued to inspire me with her accomplishments in aviation. She had a commercial license, multi-engine and instrument ratings, and she worked as a flight instructor at Merritt Island Air Service. She started her air racing career in 1974 when she and Laird flew in the Florida-Deltona Derby. The following year, she and her friend, Betty came in sixth place in the All Women's International Air Race, also known as the Angel Derby.

Women's air racing dates back to Amelia Earheart and the Women's Air Derby of 1929, the first transcontinental air race allowing female pilots to enter. Prior to the race, Amelia held a meeting of women pilots and founded the Ninety-Nines, the International Organization of Women Pilots, named for the ninety nine ladies who attended. Women had been racing planes ever since, and I wanted to be a part of it too.

The first race I entered was the 1975 Deltona Derby. The race went from Sanford to Naples and over to Marco Island, about 300 miles total. I knew racing required a few modifications to increase speed. When Bonnie raced, she closed the vents on her airplane to reduce drag, and she didn't take any baggage along, cutting excess weight. The cockpit could get very hot with the vents closed, but it was a sacrifice most pilots were willing to make.

Bob would be my co-pilot for this race, and he told me in no uncertain terms what he thought about those sacrifices. "If

I'm going to race with you, we're **not** closing the vents and we're taking our luggage with us!"

As a new pilot, I gave Bob's opinions priority over mine. With his engineering background, I assumed he knew more than me. Sometimes when I wanted to fly, he would say, "You're going flying today?"

What does he know that I don't know? I thought. I bit my tongue whenever he made comments like that. It would be much later before I challenged Bob when it came to flying, so I agreed to his demands to keep the vents open and bring along a suitcase. I was happy to be racing, and didn't expect to do well on my first try anyway. A little extra weight wouldn't make much difference.

The weatherman briefed everyone before we took off from the Sanford Airport. Since I was a novice at racing, I wanted to be well informed. I gingerly raised my hand to ask a question. "What are the winds at three, six, and nine?" referring to altitudes of three, six, and nine thousand feet.

I realized my blunder when I saw Bonnie's face. *Oh no, I've embarrassed her. I wonder what I said wrong.* She explained later that pilots fly as low as possible when racing. The air at lower altitudes has more density giving the propeller more bite and giving the airplane more speed. We never even got up to three thousand feet.

Bonnie also instructed her naïve mother on how the winner is determined, not by the first plane to finish as I first thought. Instead, each team has a handicap based on the type of aircraft and the speed it normally flies. The team that does the best at beating their plane's handicap is declared the winner.

Bonnie helped us out with all the numbers, and we prayed for a tailwind like everyone else.

Bob did a good job navigating, and in a few hours we were at the finishing point in Naples. I notified the tower from ten miles out so they could record my time as I did the required fly by. If the plane's engine is very hot from racing several hours, the pilot may choose to circle a few times prior to landing, but the official race time comes from that first fly by.

Bonnie and Laird were on the committee for this race, and they got special permission for a few planes to land on Marco Island. Bob and I landed there and went inside the little airport. When we walked by the information desk, Myra Elshner, the scorekeeper, asked if I wanted my time. "What for?" I answered. I was clueless about what to do with that information.

Bonnie was one of the first people to see the final results. When she did, she cried with joy. In spite of the extra weight of our luggage, Bob and I came in second! We received a silver platter with our names inscribed.

Bonnie explained the reason we did so well on that race was the plane's handicap. The owner's manual listed the speed very low, 119 mph at 75 percent power. I flew an average of 127 mph, giving me a score of +8 and placing me high in the rankings. I didn't fully understand the numbers yet, but placing second on my first race propelled me full throttle into air racing.

Once in a Blue Mooney

Bob's love of sports cars carried over to airplanes. Even with the great score we made on my first race, we started looking at other airplanes. Bob really liked the Mooney, considered the sports car of airplanes. The Mooney had more horsepower than my Grumman, and it had retractable gear. We saw a Mooney M20F advertised in Lakeland and asked Bonnie to fly her plane over and take a look at it. She liked what she saw, so Bob and I took a commercial flight from New York to check it out.

I did a walk around the airplane while the cigar-smoking lawyer who owned it sat in the pilot seat. "It's okay, honey. You don't have to do that."

"Oh yes, I do," I answered. I didn't appreciate his condescending attitude.
Bonnie and I took the Mooney up for a short ride, and we decided to buy it.

Bob and I signed the paperwork, and flew the plane to Merritt Island. I had to

do a couple hours of flying time and have Bonnie check me out as the instructor so I could be rated for the plane's retractable gear. As soon as Bonnie signed off on my rating, Bob and I prepared to fly the new plane back to New York.

Bob often teased me that he was going to write a book titled *Sex at 9,000 Feet* or *Once in a Blue Mooney.* As I put the Mooney into a climb, Bob kept a watchful eye on the altimeter. When we passed 9,000 feet, he looked over at me with a twinkle in his eye.

"No way!" I said with a chuckle. Little did we know, this flight was about to become memorable for a very different reason. We landed in Savannah for fuel and promptly took off and flew north. The weather had been fine, but the clouds quickly began to build. I was flying VFR, and I soon realized I should turn back to Savannah.

I radioed the tower using the phonetic alphabet for my plane's call sign. "Savannah Tower, November 68, 63 Victor, requesting to return to the airport."

"63 Victor, Roger," the tower responded. He knew by my request that I was not instrument rated and would need guidance to the runway. "Do you anticipate any problems being vectored?" he asked.

I answered with an emphatic, "No sir."

He watched me on radar and directed me to the approach. "63 Victor, ceiling is 3,000 feet; your altitude is 9,000 feet. Maintain heading and descend."

"63 Victor, Roger." I watched my instruments and asked Bob to keep looking out the window for a visual of the runway.

The tower operator continued to radio his directions. I had faith he knew what he was doing. All I could see was thick, cotton-like clouds as I descended. I reached 3,000 feet but still didn't break through the ceiling. My altimeter read 2,500 feet. Still no visibility. "Do you see anything, Bob?" I asked anxiously.

"Nothing yet."

After a few more tense seconds, Bob saw the ground at 1,800 feet. I didn't break out of the clouds until we were at 1,500 feet, but I was lined up with the runway and landed perfectly.

As the plane came to a complete stop, Bob looked at me with admiration and said, "Honey, you're one cool cookie." It meant a lot coming from a man who did everything right, and I hadn't been the least bit afraid. (It's the best thing he ever said to me besides, "Marry me.")

The Angel Derby in May of 1976 provided my first opportunity to fly in a transcontinental race. I entered as Bonnie's co-pilot. She had the required hours for this long race, but we flew my Mooney. During a newspaper interview, Bonnie quipped, "We fly my mother's airplane because she *gives* orders better than she takes them." My job as the co-pilot would be to navigate and tell Bonnie where to fly.

Each team of women wore matching outfits for the race. Bonnie and I prepared like most women do for a trip—we went shopping! America's Bicentennial was in full swing, so we chose red, white, and blue patriotic outfits. We dressed as engineers complete with red hats and overalls, and we had white pantsuits for another matching outfit. Always concerned about weight and speed, we would take only the racing clothes and our toothbrushes on board.

We flew north to Quebec City, the starting point, and did the qualifying paperwork. The judges thoroughly check pilot log books for each plane to make sure they are in stock condition with no modifications. They even painted a tiny screw connected to the carburetor with red nail polish to insure no tampering. We did a static run of the engine as high as it would go while the brakes were on to check the rpms. It was then we realized the previous owner had adjusted the mixture of the carburetor, so our engine would never reach its optimum performance according to the owner's manual. All the planes were impounded until race time. One time I forgot something in the plane, and had to be escorted by a judge to get it. They took the rules very seriously.

The route for the four-day race included stops in the historic cities of Boston, Massachusetts; Schenectady, New York; Wilmington, Delaware; Richmond, Virginia; Savannah, Georgia; and St. Augustine, Florida with Ft. Lauderdale as the final destination. Pilots had the option of deciding how much fuel they carried between stops, plus the mandatory forty-five minutes of residual fuel. We could choose to do a fly by at each point or stop for fuel. If we stopped anywhere besides the designated points, we would be disqualified. It was definitely a precise numbers game, flying with as little fuel as possible from point to point because each gallon of fuel added four pounds of weight. We flew forty-five minutes on one tank, and switched to the other one. It was important to keep the plane balanced.

I became keenly aware of the performance of my airplane, taking into account all the variables—altitude, temperature, and wind direction. However, in this first Derby with Bonnie, I was still pretty wet behind the ears.

The Derby is a VFR, daylight-only race, starting every day at sunrise and ending at sunset. We knew the exact times because we could be disqualified if we were in the air a minute after official sunset.

Bonnie taxied out to the runway, and we both listened to the radio. Take offs for the race were timed two minutes apart. About thirty seconds before it was time to go, Bonnie planted her feet on the brakes and revved the engine up to full throttle. The trick is to get as much speed as possible on the ground before lift off, then stay low to increase speed before climbing.

I had just finished my private pilot's license with the required emergency training, and Bonnie had a lot of confidence in me. "Mom, where are we?" she asked.

I was in awe of racing and too busy looking around to do my job of navigating. "How am I supposed to know?" I teased. "I'm reading my movie magazine and eating bonbons." We often teased each other during a race. In reality, both pilot and co-pilot are very busy. Bonnie and I did the pre-flight planning and carefully marked our route before the race. A four-day race meant using multiple charts. Bonnie wore a stopwatch around her neck, and we had a couple others in the cockpit. Every ten minutes I checked the flight chart against our position to keep us on course, and I recorded our times. When I finished with one chart, I threw it to the seat behind me and concentrated on the next one.

The plane's engine droned on as we zoomed over mountains, lakes, towns, and treetops. I was overwhelmed with the beauty of the country as we flew over various terrain.

When the figures were tallied at the end of the race, we came in 28th out of 64 teams, a disaster by our standards, but we had other honors. Bonnie and I were chosen to carry an envelope bearing the stamp commemorating fifty years of commercial flight, 1926-1976.

We were voted best dressed and most congenial of all the teams. That shopping trip really paid off. We also had the distinction of riding in the rumble seat of an antique Ford in a parade down Las Olas Boulevard, the jewel of Fort Lauderdale.

I felt like a kid in a candy store experiencing all these things with my daughter. We already enjoyed a wonderful mother/daughter relationship, but with our racing we became close friends as well. We raced all over the country, from Canada to Florida and the Bahamas and from Los Angeles to Acapulco. With our first women's race together, we realized the Mooney definitely was not all it was cracked up to be. I would be in the market for a faster airplane before we raced again.

Mildred Meets Pamela
A Stormy Tale

Just prior to the 1976 Angel Derby in which Bonnie and I raced, my mother, Mildred, boarded a commercial airliner for her first trip alone. My brother, Vernon, worked for Pan Am, and he got a great deal on her ticket to Guam to visit our daughter, Linda and family. Initially I considered going along, but for the price it would cost me to go to Guam, I could take the whole family to California when Linda and Jack returned.

Mother was so excited about the trip, but we had no idea she was on a collision course with Pamela—Typhoon Pamela that is. Ten years after the blizzard that stranded Jack and Linda on their honeymoon in New York, they faced another record-breaking storm. With my mother as a houseguest, they battled the elements together. I'll let my son-in-law, Jack, tell the story.

* * *

I arrived in Guam in February 1967 to work as a radar operator for the satellite tracking station on what used to be called Northwest Field. My wife, Linda, joined me a month later, and we set up housekeeping in a split-level home on the side of a steep hill. We had a panoramic view of the island, beautiful sunsets over the Pacific Ocean, and the Naval Air Station which was also used as the Guam International Airport. When Pan-American Flight 852, Boeing 747 took off

173

each evening at 6:30 heading for Hawaii, we could see the wheels go up as it flew over our house.

In the twelve years we lived in Guam, we had just one serious typhoon. In that time we only had one visitor from the States, my wife's grandmother, Mildred Henry. Weirdly enough, those two events happened at the same time.

By this time I was working as an Operations Controller, coordinating the activities of the entire tracking station. I appreciated the satellite technology allowing us to track an approaching typhoon well in advance. Linda and I knew the drill. The first step in preparing for a big storm is to eat as much perishable food as possible. We were used to stocking up on batteries, water, candles, and filling gas tanks whenever typhoon warnings went out. At the time of Mildred's visit, Linda and I had lived in Guam nine years. We had never gone beyond this stage of preparation, but that was about to change.

As we waited for further developments, we took Linda's grandmother Mildred out for some sightseeing on the island. We found a Polynesian music group with all their equipment set up on an isolated beach. The band drummed and strummed and the dancers hula-ed their hearts out. It was great for Mildred to see some island culture. Later we had dinner at a teppanyaki restaurant, a Japanese style of cooking where the diners sit around the grill while the chef cooks with an artistic flair. The festive atmosphere of our family outing kept the impending storm at bay for a while.

The day before the storm it was time to take preparations to the next level. I took any remaining perishable food to the tracking station where I worked. With its own powerhouse and large water reserve, it was supposed to be typhoon proof. The station included rooms for employees, but most people chose to find their own housing as Linda and I did. The refrigerators at these little efficiency apartments were available for employee use, so I deposited our perishables there.

With that out of the way, I turned to a few other items on the preparation checklist. I filled three 40-gallon, clean garbage cans with water and strategically placed them under downspouts. I weighted each lid with a concrete block. If the power and water were disrupted for weeks, we could use the water in the cans, then use them to collect runoff from the rain spouts. We installed the typhoon window covers that came with each house in the neighborhood.

Radio reports predicted Typhoon Pamela would pass directly over Guam the next day with winds of 100-150 miles per hour. With all our storm preparations done, we tucked in the children and said goodnight to Grandma Mildred. Outer bands of the circular storm came on shore in the middle of the night with winds of 40-50 miles an hour.

The next morning Linda and I heard Mildred in the kitchen making breakfast for everyone. She flashed a wide smile as we entered the room. "Did you hear the storm last night?" she asked. "Oh my God, I've never heard such heavy rain and strong wind! I'm so sorry you kids slept through it!"

Linda and I exchanged knowing glances. "Mildred, that was just the beginning," I explained. "The real storm won't be here for three or four more hours, and it will last past sunset."

"It's going to get worse? Are you sure?"

Following breakfast, I checked for any damage around house. The winds began to pick up by midmorning. The manager of a hydroponic farm I was helping set up stopped by to ask for my help at one of the damaged greenhouses.

"There's no sense trying to salvage anything now," I told him. "The winds are only going to get stronger. The best thing to do is go home and take care of your family." The guy agreed with my sage advice and went home.

We lost power early in the storm, and Linda went around putting spoons of ice cream in everybody's mouths. I must have missed it when I moved our perishables. In any case, the kids were happy to comply. Use it or lose it.

The winds intensified rattling the storm covers on our windows. One of the neighbor's covers ripped off his house and blew down the hill. He and his brother took his car down to get it. As soon as they got back up the hill and took it out of the trunk, the wind ripped it out of their hands and blew it right back where it was. I ventured outside to see if I could help, but the force of the wind and rain instantly blinded me. Knowing I would be drenched at this good-Samaritan task, I went back inside and stripped down to Bermuda shorts and flip flops, and put on a scuba diving mask to protect my eyes.

The rain felt like needles hitting my skin as I crawled up the hill. I took shelter near our front door, looking for my neighbor to come back. I assumed he drove his Lincoln down the hill again to retrieve the shutter.

Just then a typhoon cover ripped off our house and fell against one of the garbage cans full of water. A strong gust tore the shutter from my hands as I tried to move it. In the process, the garbage can fell over, dumped all the water, and then flew into the mist about eighty feet above the neighbor's roof.

I realized the futility of trying to reinstall storm shutters during a storm. Obviously my neighbor had already figured that out. He must've surrendered to the storm. *What am I doing out here? I thought.*

When I went back inside our house, I discovered another problem. The force of the wind was literally shaking the front door and its frame. Linda and I spent the next few hours leaning against the door in shifts and sopping up the water that seeped in. At one point, I felt a fine mist spraying my face. The rain was hitting the door with such force that it went through the wood.

Mildred insisted on taking shifts at the door too. With a towel on her head and her shoulder to the door, she remarked, "Linda, you have such a cheap door!"

The door seemed "cheap" to Mildred, but overall the house was constructed to weather severe storms. Built of steel-reinforced, poured concrete, we expected it to endure the battering of high winds. What we didn't expect was all the water seepage.

The sound of 100-mile-an-hour-wind hitting a house is fearsome. It went on for over an hour, but we somehow adapted to the sound. Gusts of 150 miles an hour added more crashing and banging. When the winds were at their highest point, the house literally shook, frightening the whole family, me included. I began to doubt the strength of our reinforced house.

The eye of the storm brought a welcome calm. During our forty-five minute break, we went outside and saw dozens of typhoon covers scattered around the neighborhood. We gathered them up and reinstalled as many as we could. I grabbed a spare and took it inside. I attached one of the covers over one office window, and backed my pick up truck up against one of them for extra protection. Darkness fell as the wind picked up again. All the typhoon covers on the south side of the house were ripped off. The truck had been blown slightly away from its position, and that window cover flew off as well. It left us with a view of the pick up during the rest of the storm. We were amazed at how the wind treated the truck. Every surge of wind lifted the passenger side of the truck onto two wheels where it teetered for a few seconds, and then it would plop back on all fours. We observed that phenomenon at least a dozen times.

Elsewhere in the house, the adults took turns stabilizing the sliding glass door on the west side of the house. The kids and I were sopping up water in the office while keeping an eye on the truck with a flashlight, hoping it wouldn't tip over and go tumbling down the hill. We couldn't have done anything about it if it did, but watching seemed to help.

Suddenly we heard a loud BAM, followed by Mildred yelling. I envisioned her flying off into the darkness, clutching the glass door. When Linda and I reached her, she was still holding onto it. She was not injured, and the sliding door was fine. The noise we heard was a flying rock smashing through a different window. With a deafening roar, wind and rain poured through the opening causing the curtains to flutter against the ceiling horizontally.

I fumbled around in the dark, placing the spare typhoon cover over the broken window. I pushed our heavy coffee table against it and sat on the table to hold the cover in place. It didn't keep out all the rain, but it protected us from flying debris.

With all that commotion, we didn't realize we were running around barefoot on broken glass. Linda yelled a warning. "Freeze! There's broken glass everywhere." She distributed everybody's shoes, and the adults used flashlights to locate and pick up the visible pieces of glass.

Finally the noise from the winds and rain subsided and we managed to get a few hours of sleep before the sun came up. The house sustained mostly water damage caused when the window broke near the end of the storm. The truck had been bounced around by the wind and most of its paint had blown off as if it was sandblasted.

I went across the street to use the neighbor's Ham radio to call Linda's parents. In just a few minutes, we connected to a radio operator in Ohio who patched us through to the Zilligs in New York. I assured my mother-in-law, Shirley, that we were fine. I learned my lesson about calling after a storm when Linda and I were stuck in a blizzard on our honeymoon. That's why I called Shirley first, and I asked her to call my parents to pass the word.

At the tracking station where I worked, the huge radome that protected the 60-foot-diameter dish was destroyed, and the dish itself severely damaged. Pieces of debris from the radome fell on the cars parked in the compound, destroying every one of them. The station was off the air for three months.

Categorized as a super typhoon, Pamela destroyed 80% of the buildings on Guam with winds clocked up to 207 miles per hour. The storm dropped 33 inches of rain, making May 1976 the wettest on record. Clean up took months. President Gerald Ford declared Guam a major disaster area paving the way for millions of dollars in aid for the island. Wooden homes destroyed by the storm were eventually replaced by the concrete homes like ours. When put to the test, it kept us safe. As soon as a flight out of Guam became available, we said goodbye to Grandma Mildred. We were forever bonded by our battle with Typhoon Pamela.

* * *

My mother's trip to Guam in 1976 was marked by many firsts. She took her first flight alone and survived a typhoon. On her way home, she did some sightseeing in Hawaii. Although she was 78 years old and by herself, she took a 25-cent bus ride to tour the Arizona Memorial at the site of the 1941 attack on Pearl Harbor. She arrived home safely with incredible memories, undaunted by her run in with Typhoon Pamela.

The Cruddy Mess
Housewarming Party

Bob and I loved spending time in Ft. Lauderdale where my parents retired. We weren't ready to retire, so in the late 70s we tried running our Jiffy-tite business from Florida. I did the bookkeeping from home and Bob traveled back and forth to New York to keep tabs on things.

We had some investment property in Ft. Lauderdale not far from my parents' home, so we started out in one of those duplexes.

We often went boating in Florida and admired the homes we saw on the water. One day Bob said, "Come on honey. Let me show you the house we're going to buy." It was in a pie-shaped cul de sac with 129 feet on the Intracoastal and 129 feet on a canal, a beautiful location. The realtor said it was a good time to buy because it was about to be repossessed. The bank had given the family three months to sell it, and they were down to the last two weeks of the third month.

The original list price was $300,000, but the house was in bad shape and the sellers were pretty desperate. Going by the realtor's advice, we put in a ridiculous offer of $125,000, the value of the property alone. Judging by the shape of the house, Bob planned to tear it down and rebuild anyway.

The sellers didn't accept our offer, so the realtor asked if we could go up a couple thousand dollars because there was another buyer. Bob joked with the real estate agent, "We'll have to count our pennies. I guess my wife could sell her airplane if we have to."

We were thrilled when the seller took our second offer. We found out later that daredevil motorcyclist Evel Kineval had offered to pay $10,000 more than the asking price, but he wanted his children "swimming in the pool by the weekend." I guess he thought money could fix anything quickly. Kineval was at the peak of his career at that time. He had attempted his biggest stunt in 1974, jumping the Snake River Canyon in his Skycycle.

He ended up buying a house in another Ft. Lauderdale neighborhood. We heard he went up and down the street telling the neighbors, "I'm Evel Kineval and I'm going to buy this house. If you don't like all my trucks around, I'll buy you all out."

Our Fort Lauderdale dream home

Besides getting a great deal, we enjoyed beating out a celebrity. Instead of bulldozing, we decided to remodel the house.

182

We were excited to get started, and our friends couldn't wait to see the new place.

Steven and a buddy came down for a visit, so we hosted a party at the house before we did anything to it. The owners left some furniture there, and the whole house was a mess. We walked into the living room and saw a screwdriver on the floor among other things. "Leave it there," I said. "We'll put a new twist on the normal housewarming party. Let's have a cruddy mess cocktail party."

I bought canning jars for our drinks and used a mop bucket for ice. Paint trays covered with saran wrap displayed the hors d'oeuvres. Bob planned to wear a white t-shirt and jeans for the party, but the day of the party he decided the white shirt looked too clean. He went outside to dirty it up. He found a puddle from the rain we had the night before, so he bent down and scooped up some dirty water and patted it all over his shirt. After a few tries he stood up to look at his handiwork and heard someone call his name.

"Mr. Zillig? I'm your next-door neighbor." With a sheepish grin, Bob explained his actions and invited the man to the party. Our neighbor wasn't afraid to introduce himself to a grown man playing in the mud, and we became good friends after the meeting by the puddle.

* * *

While we were in the midst of our Ft. Lauderdale house remodel, Bonnie flew in the 1977 Angel Derby with co-pilot, Betty Dodds and won the race. Although I was very busy decorating our Ft. Lauderdale home, I flew whenever I could. Soon I had the 200 required hours for a commercial license.

I wanted the license to be a better pilot. In addition to that, I could carry passengers for hire if I wanted to. I did the required ground school for the commercial license in Buffalo. The final step was to fly my check ride, a pass or fail test of pilot skill.

The day of my check ride was very windy, but I was grateful. I could blame the bumpy ride on the wind and not my flying. My instructor, Jack Prior, came in sneezing and wiping his nose. I could tell he didn't feel well, but I hoped it wouldn't affect my grade on the flight.

On a check ride, the pilot flies to a certain point and then comes back. The instructor might try to get you lost and ask you to return to the airport, or he might remove a fuse so you wouldn't have a fuel gauge. The pilot is never sure what the instructor might ask her to do or what they might do *to* her.

I did everything Jack told me to do, then waited to hear from the tower so I could return to the airport. After a while Jack asked, "Well, when are you going to turn around?" I knew I had followed procedure in waiting for the radio call, but they had forgotten me. I called them again to ask how long I should fly in that direction. They gave me a heading to return to the airport. After Jack's comment I thought I had failed the check ride.

When we landed I went into the airport shaking and waited for the results. Jack came in and told the girl at the desk, "She passed."

My feeling of dread turned to surprise followed by joy. *I better make a quick exit in case he changes his mind.*

* * *

One summer day in 1977, Bob and I were driving around Olcott, New York. We saw a seven-foot-tall suit of armor outside an antique shop. The imposing figure dwarfed the size of an actual knight. I thought it would look great in the foyer of our Ft. Lauderdale home, so I gladly paid the $75 for it. *What a great deal*, I thought.

Bob threw cold water on my excitement when he asked, "How are you going to get that thing to Florida?"

I hadn't thought of that. We made some calls to see if we could ship it somehow. Nobody could help us. Then I had a brilliant idea. If I had a larger airplane, we could do it. Bob understood my reasoning since he had used it when buying his last boat. "For a few dollars more," I bought a six-seater Cherokee Lance. We were in the market for a faster airplane anyway after the Mooney did such a terrible job in the air race. Now we had another excuse for an upgrade. Bob and I removed the back seats and jiggled the knight until it laid down for the flight from New York to Florida.

I named the knight Max and stationed him as a sentry in the foyer of our Ft. Lauderdale home. Years later when we moved to Merritt Island he came along. We strapped Max onto the bumper of a big truck for the move. I'm sure other motorists were taken by surprise at the sight of a suit of armor facing them riding down the road. Every time we moved, Max went with us, and he remains a guardian of my home.

Dallas Dilly Dally
The 1978 Angel Derby

In the spring of 1978, Bonnie and I teamed up once again for the Angel Derby, now called the All Women's International Air Race. Bonnie had a Cherokee 6, and I had traded in my Mooney for a bigger airplane too. It was a high-performance airplane with retractable gear and a variable-pitch propeller. That meant the pitch of the prop's blades could be adjusted based on the wind direction allowing the plane to fly faster.

Bonnie had an ATP (Airline Transport Pilot) license by this time, which required 1,500 hours, and I was working on my instrument rating. With my new plane and our combined flying experience, we expected to do well in the race.

Bonnie and I did the traditional prep work, studying the charts and shopping for a new wardrobe of matching outfits. The airplane got spa treatment as we polished  her for the race. The shinier the airplane, the faster she flies.

Before we left for Dallas, we removed two of the back seats in the airplane, hoping to lighten the load. The judges had a different opinion. I found out the hard way that stock condition meant I couldn't race unless all six seats were in place. No matter how I argued, the judges stayed firm in their decision. "Put the seats back or you're out." We made a quick call to Bob who put the seats on a plane to Dallas.

We had no problem waiting for the seats to arrive, because the start of the race was delayed. The rules dictated the race couldn't begin unless weather conditions were good all the way to the first stop, Hot Springs, Arkansas. All 41 teams of women were stuck in Dallas with nothing to do. We had to be ready to go by sunrise the next morning, even if we were not sure the weather had improved. It didn't, and we were delayed a total of a day and a half. The race finally started at 3:30 the afternoon of May 7.

With the seat problem and weather delays, we still had something to be happy about. Bonnie drew the number one slot in the starting line up.

A fierce competitor now, I was willing to do whatever it took to win. We practically raced in our underwear. Closing the vents in the airplane made the cockpit unbearably hot, so we would remove our blouses and sponge down with a damp cloth every so often. We kept a small container of water for that purpose and another one served as a portable potty for emergencies.

It's not something lady pilots like to talk about—bathrooming in the air. Bonnie and I took this into consideration when shopping for our flying wardrobe. The popular jumpsuits of the seventies were out of the question.

Men don't have to think about potty breaks; they can use a pilot's relief tube, as they call it, and keep flying. We had a contraption called a Jill-John. It had a "bladder" attached to a very long hose. It fits into a decorative purse-like case, so when you leave the airplane, nobody knows what you're carrying.

One time as I was using the little port-a-john, I was struggling to get into position. As I moved around, the plane began banking to the left and right as Bonnie tried to help me. "Is everything all right?" we heard over the radio. We were close enough for the tower to have a visual, and they noticed our wings rocking. I don't remember how we answered, but we lied.

Just like a family on a long road trip, Bonnie and I sometimes sang as we raced. We'd sing a song related to every state we flew over, "The Red River Valley" or "California, Here I Come" to name a few. When we went through Arkansas in the 1978 race, I tried to remember the tune to "The Arkansas Traveler." (It's the same one as "I'm Bringing Home a Baby Bumblebee.") We called the tower and asked if any of them knew it. They asked around, but nobody did. It was a silly thing to ask on the radio, but the tradition added some levity during hours of flight.

By the time we arrived at the Nashville stop, we had a 34-point advantage over my plane's 193-mph handicap. Weather delayed us again on the second leg of the trip, and we fought headwinds as we flew south to Florida. Our 34-point rating dropped to a plus ten over our handicap.

The next morning we took off from Ft. Myers in beautiful weather and flew to Freeport, Bahamas, making up some of our loss. It wasn't enough to catch the leaders though, and we came in sixth place, only a five-hundredth of a mile behind the team in fifth place.

* * *

Business was doing well as we approached the fall of 1978 and our 35th wedding anniversary. So well, in fact, that one of our employees took a trip to Hawaii. I couldn't help it. I was a bit jealous. I told Bob, "If the help can afford a trip to Hawaii, why can't we?"

"You want to go to Hawaii, honey? Let's do it," came Bob's ready reply.

We booked our tickets on a group tour, but while we were there, we spent most of the time off by ourselves. One evening at dinner, another lady in our group approached us. "Do you mind if I ask you a personal question?" she asked. "How long have you been married?"

"Thirty-five years," I answered as I smiled at Bob.

"We noticed the way you two are together, and we were practically taking bets you were newlyweds," the woman explained. "That's wonderful."

She didn't have to tell me. I loved every minute I was married to my sweet husband.

Flying With Living Legends

After racing in two women's air races and joining the Ninety-Nines, the female pilot's organization, I had met several living legends. I raced with women who were pioneers in female aviation, yet they put me at ease and even knew my name.

One such lady was Edna Gardner Whyte. She started flying in the 1930s when women still found it difficult to get a pilot's license. She trained thousands of military pilots during World War II and beyond, and she financed and built two airports, one of them when she was in her seventies. She earned many awards and accomplished much in the field of aviation.

Edna was a past president of the Ninety-Nines, and they wanted to honor her at the completion of the 1978 race. The race committee asked me to fly Edna and her nurse from St. Petersburg, Florida to the Bahamas. To say I was nervous would be an understatement. How could I fly for a pilot with her expertise?

I did my checklists as always, and the flight was perfect, right online with navigation, altitude and radio work. According to my instructions, I did a low fly by and then came in for a landing in Freeport. I couldn't have felt more honored if I flew for the President in Air Force One.

Jerrie Cobb was another famous lady pilot and former astronaut trainee I met in the Ninety-Nines. Jerrie and I were both members of the Spaceport Chapter.

Jerrie had already set aviation records and won several awards when she was chosen in 1959 to be the first female to undergo astronaut testing. She passed with flying colors and could have become the first woman in space.

As history records, that was not to be. In 1962 NASA decided America was not ready for female astronauts. A year later the Russians sent the first woman into space, and it was many more years before American women could join the astronaut ranks. Jerrie went on to use her flying skills in mission work to the Amazon jungle for many years. Our Spaceport Chapter of the Ninety-Nines collected blankets and sneakers for Jerrie's foundation, and I was glad to contribute.

Following John Glenn's return to space in the late 1990s, Jerrie had great support as she sought a position as a somewhat mature female astronaut. She was denied that opportunity as well, but she remains a wonderful role model for female aviators.

Even though I was in awe of the many experienced female pilots I raced with, they were still my rivals. When Bonnie and I raced together with my Tiger Grumman, we had the audacity to toilet paper a competitor's airplane and post a sign on it saying, "You've Got a Tiger on Your Tail." The rival was Margaret Ringenberg, and I'm sure she had no trouble figuring out who did the deed.

Margaret's flying career began as a ferry pilot with the Women Air force Service Pilots or WASPs during World War II. Although women weren't allowed to fly into combat, Margaret's duties were often dangerous. Besides being a test pilot, she towed targets for pilots in training, which meant she could easily become the target. Following the war she flew as a commercial pilot and instructor. She raced in every Powder Puff Derby from 1957 and continued racing when it was changed to the Air Race Classic in 1977. Margaret competed in races well into her seventies, including the Round-the-World Air Race at the age of 72. A full chapter is devoted to Margaret in Tom Brokaw's book, *The Greatest Generation*.

I'm sure none of her accolades entered my mind as I strung yards of toilet paper around the wings and propeller of her airplane. Bonnie and I had a great laugh out of it, and Margaret was a good sport. We became friends, and she and her husband visited Bob and I once when they were in Florida. When I knew her, Margaret looked like a soft-spoken grandmother who just happened to have decades of flying experience.

She flew most of her life, completing her last race in 2008 at the age of 87, just one month before she passed away. Always willing to share her flying experiences with others, she was in Oshkosh representing the WASPs at the Experimental Aircraft Association (EAA) air show. It was an appropriate final flight for this distinguished aviatrix.

Science fiction author, Marty Caidin, is another person on my list of living legends. We met through his wife, Dee Dee, another member of the Ninety-Nines. Marty's book, *The Cyborg*, became the well-known TV series, "The Six Million Dollar Man." Besides his love of science fiction, Marty had a passion for flying. He purchased and restored Hitler's plane, a Junker II. One day I saw it sitting at the airport in Homestead, Florida as he prepared to fly it in an air show. Dee Dee waved her arms at me and called out, "Shirley! Come on!"

Without a second's hesitation, I dashed for the plane and climbed in through the door on its underbelly. Bob saw my legs disappear into the fuselage of the plane and we took off. What a great thrill to fly around in a World War II airplane with a famous writer and pilot!

My membership in the Ninety-Nines brought me into a league of pilots of which I would never have dreamed. It was wonderful to be part of an organization of female pilots that supports and promotes a passion for flight and its safety.

Shut Up! I'm Flying the Plane!

In the late seventies, Bob and I were still running Jiffy-tite. We had a home in Ft. Lauderdale, one in Clarence, New York, and our little vacation cottage in Olcott. With all our moving around, it was impossible for me to be in one place long enough to take the twelve-week ground school to get my instrument rating.

I thought I could get around the obstacle by attending weekend classes and taking the test. The first time I did, I scored seventy-four percent, a hair under the required seventy-five to pass. On the second try, my grade dropped to seventy. *This isn't good*, I thought. *I have to change how I'm doing things.*

For my third attempt, I stayed at the hotel where the class was held. When I wasn't in class, I studied. I studied and studied some more. The afternoons were the worst. I went out for lunch and came back at 1:00 with a full stomach, a condition that defeated my concentration. Besides that, they taught the most boring section in the afternoons—weather. It took all my effort just to stay awake.

I persevered for my third set of weekend classes and took the test. When I got my score, I couldn't believe it. A sixty-nine! How could I study so much and fail again? I called Bob to tell him my depressing news. "I will be afraid to fly on a sunny day," I griped.

After that letdown, I regrouped and analyzed my situation. Obviously I couldn't master the material by taking weekend classes, but how would I ever have the time to take a twelve-week class?

My answer came when a six-week concentrated course was offered in Ft. Lauderdale. I signed up and put in my time, ever hopeful for a passing grade. At the end of the course I earned an eighty-nine percent. *That's more like it. I know I'm a good pilot.*

Statistics say instrument-rated pilots increase their flying time to seventy percent. With a VFR license, the pilot is subject to the weather, affecting your flying capability about half of the time because there is always bad weather somewhere. With my instrument rating, I could fly in conditions that would have grounded me before.

There was another perk to getting my instrument rating that I didn't realize at first. As I mentioned earlier, I relinquished my pilot-in-command status whenever Bob questioned my flying. That changed one day as I came in for a landing. Bob seemed irritated and asked, "Don't you think you're coming in too high?"

"Shut up! I'm flying this plane," I snapped.

He did shut up, and I felt vindicated. I finally felt I knew more than he did about flying, and I had the paperwork to prove it. My new confidence at the controls made me a better pilot, and Bob didn't mind when I put him in his place. In fact, he was very proud of me, and continued to empty his pockets on my flying habit.

I found a way to help compensate for Bob's empty pockets. I would lease my airplane. I didn't realize at the time this was risky business. One day a fellow named Paul contacted me about renting my airplane. He said he wanted to take his family to Georgia to see his grandmother. He did file a flight plan to Georgia, but he never arrived there. When my plane didn't show up, the FAA called me saying it was missing. They later found the abandoned plane in the Bahamas, and put the pieces of the story together.

Paul had flown there on a drug run. When he landed, he saw the police sitting at the end of the runway. As he tried to brake to a stop, he ground looped the plane, damaging the propeller, and he took off running. The plane at that point was not too severely damaged. In fact one of my pilot friends who had a plane just like mine told me later that she saw it at the airport in Nassau. "If I'd known it was your plane, I could have flown it back for you," she explained.

Before I could recover the airplane and get the propeller fixed, another shady fellow named George took advantage of me. My airplane was found sitting in his junkyard warehouse. The serial numbers verified my ownership. George told me by phone the plane wasn't flyable, but he would offer me $4,000 for the remains. What an outlandish figure for a plane worth $90,000. After his ridiculous offer we referred to this unscrupulous man as $4,000 George.

We recovered the Lance from George's warehouse and had it shipped back to Miami in a cargo plane. I sobbed when I saw it. The outside looked like someone bashed every inch of it with a sledge hammer. The inside had been gutted and all the seats removed except the pilot's. The 300-horsepower engine had been removed, but it was sent back with the plane.

I was devastated with the loss of my plane. It was the only time I had a drink before noon. If the loss wasn't enough, I still had to argue with the insurance company for the claim. They said I was insured for the Caribbean but not the Bahamas. I didn't take that lying down. I hired my own adjuster, to prove the Bahamas was part of the Caribbean. The company paid $75,000 on the claim, and I still had to pay my lawyer.

As we researched the whole episode, we learned that Paul tried to rent a plane from the Pompano Airport, but he didn't have the required hours logged to fly across the Caribbean to the Bahamas. I felt so violated by the authorities in Pompano who never alerted anyone in Ft. Lauderdale. They knew he would try to rent a plane there. They argued it would have constituted defamation of character to say anything about Paul, but it was okay to allow the guy to rip off a grandmother.

I didn't want to fly in such a damaged craft again, so I counted my losses and sold the plane for parts. I felt defrocked as a pilot with no airplane to fly. Once I recovered from the ordeal, Bob and I started looking for another airplane. We found a ten-year-old Piper Cherokee 235 advertised in Trade-A-Plane. After checking on it by phone, Bob and I flew to Tennessee to pick it up. I was happy to be an airplane owner again.

FIRST WOMEN'S AIR DERBY
50th ANNIVERSARY
COMMEMORATIVE RACE

Angel Derby
1979 RACE ROUTE

AUGUST 21·22·23·24·25
2,714.2 STATUTE MILES

1979 RACE

Bonnie and I decided I would be the pilot in command for the next Angel Derby—The First Women's Air Derby 50th Anniversary Commemorative Race in August 1979. We would start in Santa Monica, California and retrace the route of the First Women's Transcontinental Air Race of 1929. There were many stops along the way in 1929 because the airplanes didn't have the capacity to fly great distances. Rules for the race would be different than in previous Derbies. Instead of doing fly bys at some of our stops, we were required to touchdown at each one. It was a long 2,700-mile race lasting five days and ending in Cleveland, Ohio in time for the annual air show.

The race officials pre-visited all the cities on the route, so reporters from the local papers were waiting for us at each stop. Conditions at our landing sites varied as we flew across the country. One small airfield in Texas had grass growing on the runway.

Bonnie and I each donned vintage headgear to commemorate the race and pilots of 1929. Mine be-

longed to my father when he flew as a test pilot at Consolidated Aircraft, and I wished he were there to see me fly.

The Ryan Storm Scope is a weather instrument that shows precipitation and updates every thirty seconds. It is an expensive addition to any cockpit, so before buying one I wrote a lovely letter to the company asking if we could represent them in the races. I was hoping to get a free scope. They didn't take my offer, so I paid the $7,000 and got the scope anyway. It was the best instrument I ever had, and I never regretted spending the money for it.

If we saw some storm clouds ahead, the scope showed an opening to get through. During one race we flew through a section in the Midwest where the sky was black. Some of the teams were stuck a day or so because of the storm, but my scope allowed me to fly safely through it.

With so many stops on the route, I pulled out my credit card more often for fuel and other expenses. One day the Texaco Company called Bob to alert him. "Mr. Zillig, have you lost your credit card? We see  charges on your card all across the country."

"Oh, that's just my wife," he explained. "She's flying in a cross-country race."

Bonnie and I made good time, but on the final leg of the race the plane started shaking. I had just cleared the Mansfield, Ohio tower, but called them back in case we had to return. The cockpit gauges looked good, so we weren't sure what was causing the airplane to shake. I decided to keep flying. We were so close to finishing the race.

Neither Bonnie nor I said anything, but we both knew we had a serious problem. We silently worked out plans to ditch the plane if it came to that. Bonnie looked down and saw sailboats racing on Lake Erie. *One of them can rescue us if we end up in the water,* she thought. I focused on the shore and planned to glide to a landing since it wasn't that far and the terrain was pretty flat. Thankfully, we didn't have to implement our plan.

As we flew around cooling the engine, we hit two seagulls. I couldn't avoid them, and they smacked into the airplane, denting the leading edge of the wing. We let out a collective sigh of relief when we landed.

All the pilots lined up for a picture, and we got back in the plane to taxi to the hangar. It wouldn't start, but we thanked God the engine hadn't quit until we were on the ground. He certainly watched over us. The engine trouble slowed us down, putting us in third place for that very grueling race.

I found out I had leaned the engine a little too much by pulling back on the throttle for speed and distance. That aerates the fuel more and makes the engine work harder. One of the cylinders stuck. When they worked on the engine they found metal chips from the cylinder in the oil.

They towed my airplane to the hangar and parked it next to the plane of one of the top aerobatic pilots of the day. He was there for the Cleveland National Air Show following our race, and I felt honored to share hangar space with his airplane.

We got my plane running so I could fly the short hop home to Buffalo. I had thrown away all the charts we used during the race, but I remembered all the tower frequencies from Cleveland to Buffalo. I flew along the shore of Lake Erie and had no trouble getting home.

Following the race, I opted to get a new engine instead of refurbishing the one I had. That turned out to be a mistake. Not only did it cost more, my plane never flew as fast again.

The Flying Fruit Salad

Bonnie and I looked forward to our next race in a new decade. We signed up for the 1980 Air Race Classic, the successor to the Powder Puff Derby sponsored by the Ninety-Nines organization. When the Derby experienced financial trouble in 1977, a new board formed which included many of the same women from the Ninety-Nines. The same pilots who raced in the Powder Puff Derby continued to compete in the Air Race Classic. Bonnie and I had never flown in the Powder Puff Derby, and this would be our first time competing in the Air Race Classic.

Aside from its long history of famous female pilots, the Powder Puff Derby was immortalized in a rather unusual way. Jean Schultz, wife of cartoonist Charles Schultz, and her mother flew as a team in the 1975 race and inspired Schultz to write about it in his *Peanuts* comic strip.

Cartoon characters Marcie and Peppermint Patty traced the same route as the real contestants—Riverside, California to Boyne Falls, Michigan. They flew in a rented plane, Snoopy's Sopwith camel, and they referred to him as the mechanic. Unfortunately, Snoopy reneged on his rental agreement and took back his doghouse, or should I say, airplane so he could fly a World War I mission over France. Peppermint Patty was outraged that a stupid dog cost her the race.

In writing his comic strip, Schultz forgot to dress Marcie and Patty alike. Matching wardrobes for the female flying teams was a necessity, and it made for some funny stories as we stayed at hotels in each city on the racing routes.

One day Bonnie and I wore matching t-shirts with a pilot-uniform design on the front. We went over to a sign-in table for a wedding reception at our hotel. "We're the pilots for the bride and groom's private jet," Bonnie teased.

"Just a minute," The lady manning the table disappeared and came back with the bride and groom. We introduced ourselves, and the couple got such a kick out of our joke they invited us to join the party.

Another time, somebody thought Bonnie and I belonged to the twins' convention being held at our hotel. Bonnie's friend and former co-pilot, Betty, told another story about a conversation she heard in a hotel elevator. "I wonder why all those women are dressed in pairs," said a lady.

"Maybe it's a conference for lesbians," the other woman offered.

I'd rather be mistaken for my daughter's twin than a lesbian, but either way, the women pilots always drew lots of attention.

Every year Bonnie and I enjoyed shopping for our wardrobe before each race. One year we won a $5,000 prize, but we probably spent $6,000 on our expenses for fuel, hotels, and clothes. It never seemed to balance out, but the experiences we had were priceless. Bob gladly supported me financially, but as the 1980 race approached, someone suggested we ask Florida designer Lilly Pulitzer to sponsor us. We were living in Ft. Lauderdale, not far from Lilly's headquarters, and we loved her clothes. It sounded like a great idea.

Lilly's story as a designer began when she eloped with Peter Pulitzer and came to Palm Beach, Florida. She opened a juice stand in 1959 using citrus from her husband's groves. Lilly noticed a lot of juice stains on her clothes, so she made a sleeveless shift out of some brightly-printed cotton. It wasn't long and her customers became enamored with her clothes. She began selling more dresses than juice.

When her former schoolmate, Jacqueline Bouvier Kennedy, wore a *Lilly* on vacation in 1962, her picture appeared in Life Magazine. American women wanted anything the First Lady wore, and they went crazy for Lilly's designs. Suddenly Lilly Pulitzer creations were in high demand with socialites and celebrities, and her clothing line skyrocketed.

As we entered the 80s, Lilly Pulitzer resort wear was still very popular. The Florida-friendly, colorful clothes were perfect for Bonnie and me. I was so excited when Lilly agreed to sponsor us that I had my airplane painted in bright orange, yellow and green with matching lime-green upholstery.

My grandchildren called it the flying fruit salad, and the red night beacon became the cherry on top.

I found some orange, yellow and green sandals to match the plane's color scheme. I even made propeller covers out of a bright, floral fabric. Why not make everything a fashion statement?

Bonnie and I thought we were dreaming as we walked up and down the aisles in Lilly's warehouse choosing our FREE wardrobe. It was a shopping spree unmatched in the history of female aviation. We chose floral skirts, pink blouses and lime-green blazers for one of our matching outfits.

We never met Lilly personally, but we spoke on the phone and she sent us a telegram the day before the race began in Corpus Christi, Texas. "Darling girls," she wrote. "I know the skies will never be the same. We are counting on your victory."

With the plane's facelift and our designer wardrobe, Bonnie and I were ready to fly. We usually flew the race route backwards to check out terrain and the airports in each city. Reporters in West Virginia, South Carolina, Illinois, and Kansas took pictures and wrote articles about Bonnie and me as we traveled the week before the race. When we arrived in Fort Smith, Arkansas where we planned to spend the night, a surprise awaited us. There was "no room at the inn."

A massive Cuban exodus into Florida began two months earlier, but its affects reached us in Arkansas as well. The Mariel Boatlift started in April of 1980. Over 125,000 Cubans were given freedom to leave Mariel Harbor from April to October. People from Miami took hundreds of small boats to pick up the refugees. The boats were usually overloaded, and the U.S. Coast Guard intervened saving thousands of lives. It was the biggest operation in peacetime history for the Coast Guard.

President Carter allowed the Cuban immigrants entrance into the U.S. without papers. This became political suicide for him because Castro released prisoners and mental patients among the refugees. The influx of exiles overwhelmed south Florida, and we felt the impact as residents of Fort Lauderdale. When the crime rate increased, so did public outcry. The U.S. started sending some of the Cubans to processing centers around the country, one of which was Fort Chaffee, just outside of the city of Fort Smith, Arkansas.

When Bonnie and I flew into the airport, we found out we would have to drive 25 miles to find a room. Thousands of Cuban immigrants filled up the local hotels, and we had to look elsewhere. It amazed us that the Mariel Boatlift still affected us so far from home.

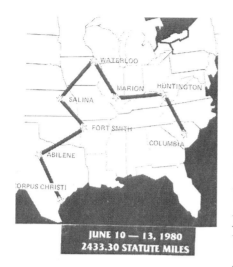

JUNE 10 — 13, 1980
2433.30 STATUTE MILES

We began our 2,400-mile race the morning of June 10 as we flew out of Corpus Christi, Texas. We zig-zagged across the country stopping in Arkansas, Kansas, Illinois and finally ending in Columbia, South Carolina. Despite my plane's fancy paint job and our designer wardrobe, Bonnie and I finished 20th out of 45 planes. We gambled with the weather in waiting for tailwinds that never materialized, but the greatest prize remained our time flying together.

The Angels Fly to Mexico

The Angel Derby of 1981 was a racing vacation. This time the President and organizer of the All Women's International Air Race, Virginia Britt, had garnered the sponsorship of the Mexican Tourism Office. They put up $10,000 to be divided for the top three prizes. We would start in Van Nuys, California, fly along the Pacific coast of Mexico, and finish in Acapulco, 1,729 statue miles.

Our trip began when we flew from Florida to Buffalo, New York to attend Steven and Barbie's wedding. The next leg of the trip took us cross-country to California to visit Linda and Jack and the kids. Bonnie and I spent a few days with them before continuing south to the starting point of the race in Los Angeles.

Flying into L.A. was a challenge because of the way the fog rolls in. With those conditions, I thought every pilot that flew there should be instrument rated. Our first stop in Mexico was Mexicali where we cleared customs. We felt very welcomed with a big banquet, margaritas, and mariachis playing. We took precautions, taking a vial of water-purifying tablets so we could brush our teeth. One of the teams had to drop out when they got the dreaded Monteczuma's revenge.

Much of the race we flew over the beautiful aqua water of the Pacific. We could fly at even lower altitudes than we did in our other races, and we felt like birds as the plane skimmed along the shining surf of Mexico's west coast.

We enjoyed the lower fuel prices in Mexico, but we had to stop at every point to make sure we had enough. The charts we normally used for flying were called sectionals, but in Mexico they had WAC charts (World Avionics Charts) which were less detailed. We were flying along and Bonnie pointed. "See that mountain over there, Mom? It's not on the chart."

We spent our first night of the race in Mazatlan. The hotel room had a balcony with flowers cascading down. The beauty and fragrance of that place was intoxicating, but we were up before dawn the next day to continue on to gorgeous Puerto Vallarta. As I looked over to the shore, I saw solid pine trees. I thought of Bob and his love of sailing as we flew over the picturesque coastline. How he would love to be on that water!

The terrain became somewhat mountainous as we flew over Zihuatanejo and on to our final destination of Acapulco. Not only did we enjoy this very different race, but we also came in second place.

Bonnie, Bob and I posing with our second place trophy.

211

When the race was over, we became tourists in the truest sense.

Bob and Laird each booked tickets to Acapulco so they could be there to surprise Bonnie and me. The only problem was Bob's travel agent neglected to tell him about some documents he needed. He didn't fly directly to Acapulco, and upon landing in Mexico, the authorities came on board to check paperwork. Bob didn't understand the stream of Spanish as they took him off the plane, but he knew he was in trouble. Somehow he talked his way out of it and was allowed to continue on to Acapulco. He still didn't have the proper papers to fly home. Virginia, the race's organizer, knew some people in Acapulco that helped us out, and Bob got what he needed.

We spent three days in Acapulco following the race. It was so much fun to have my husband at the finish line to celebrate with me. We rented one of the jeeps and drove up the beach to go parasailing. My wish for Bob to sail the beautiful coast of Mexico came true as we glided above sparkling waters. It gave me another perspective on the terrain I had just flown over in the race.

We all went into a restaurant one night with a goat tied up out front. Laird always liked to order something native to the country, and we joked with him when we saw goat on the menu. We couldn't wait to see if the goat was still tied up outside when we left.

Our little vacation came to an end all too quickly. Bob and Laird flew home commercially, and Bonnie and I flew my plane back. Some of the other women fueled their planes the night before so they could get an early start. The next morning somebody's gas had been drained, and another lady's plane had the oil drained. The planes were supposedly in a protected compound, but their idea of security left us wondering. The taxis there used the same octane we did in our planes. Bonnie and I fueled in the morning, so we avoided those issues.

I flew north across Mexico's peninsula to Tampico and on to Matamoros near the border where we fueled once more before leaving the country. We flew a few more minutes to cross the border and touched down in Brownsville, Texas to clear customs. We flew at a higher altitude than we were used to in order to clear mountain peaks and were concerned about our oxygen levels. Pilots are required to have oxygen if they fly more than a half hour above 12,500 feet. Bonnie and I took turns writing our names as a way to check for the effects of hypoxia, oxygen deficiency, and our penmanship seemed fine to us. By the time we got to Houston I was nauseous and had a headache, symptoms of altitude sickness. I didn't realize living in Florida at sea level could make me so sensitive to high altitudes.

Not only did I feel rotten, I realized when we landed in Houston that I didn't have my credit card. I called Bob immediately and told him I left my card in Mexico and he needed to cancel it. The next day Bonnie flew the rest of the way home while I sipped orange juice and struggled to feel better. When we landed I wanted nothing more than to climb into my bed.

Once recuperated, I enjoyed reliving the Mexican race with Bonnie as we looked at the snapshots and shared stories with the whole family.

Our trip took a total of 31 days, and we logged 32,000 miles in my plane. We joked about my credit card smoking from all the use. Even though I had left it in Mexico, I didn't expect any Mexicans to try to pass as a blond woman named Zillig.

Months later we got a call from the credit card company. The card turned up in North Carolina. We figured someone in Mexico sold it and it circulated back to the states, a residual sign that the angels and our derby had been in Mexico.

A Flying Entrepreneur

Flying with a sponsor in the 1980 race helped out with our wardrobe expenses, but it didn't offset the costs of fuel, hotels, and food. Hubby's wallet and our Jiffy-Tite company still served as the piggy bank for my flying hobby. I wanted to find a way to write off some of my airplane expenses. One of my pilot girlfriends, Betty D., had an air taxi service she wanted to sell. I thought that would work perfectly, so we made the deal. I set up an office at the Ft. Lauderdale Airport, put an ad in the phone book, and I took over Safe Air International.

I kept Betty on as my chief pilot, and I did all the paperwork. I had the credentials to fly commercially in the States, but not across the water to the Bahamas.

One time we had a client that chartered a jet to fly him across to Nassau. I brokered a model 24 Lear jet and a pilot, and Betty flew right seat on the way over. We charged the client

On the phone at my air service, Safe Air International

about $3,000, and I thought it was suspicious when he paid us in $20 bills. All the drug runners got their money in twenties. When we dropped the client off, I jumped in the co-pilot seat for a little experience flying a jet. It climbed like a homeward angel. In less than three minutes we were at 41,000 feet. What an experience! When we neared the final approach to the Ft. Lauderdale Airport, the pilot took over. It was the only time I had my hands on the yoke of a private jet, and it felt great.

Betty and I came up with a promotional idea for my air taxi business—Mystery Dinner Flights. We booked groups of four people for an evening flight to a nice restaurant. The fee included a champagne flight, dinner, and dessert. The passengers didn't know where we were going to take them—it was a mystery. The fun part was when Betty and I went around the area to check out places for the mystery flights.

On one of our trips, we went to the west coast of Florida and stopped near Betty's parents' home. Betty suggested we stay the night with her folks and fly back the next day. Betty knew her parents didn't smoke or drink, and for some reason they didn't have ice cubes either. Betty came prepared though. We were in our robes getting comfortable after our trip when she asked her mother for some ice water. She had none, so Betty said, "Let's go get some ice, Shirley."

We drove to a convenience store and bought a bag of ice, then Betty pulled a suitcase out of the trunk and opened it up. Inside were the makings of our drinks complete with lemon wedges in a Tupperware container. We sat in the car in our robes having cocktails, then went back to being house guests. The next morning Betty's parents fed us a huge breakfast and sent us on our way.

We only booked a few Mystery Dinner Flights, so we discontinued them. I was glad that I had a regular contract with a business that put tuna towers on boats. The aluminum framework had a high seat so fishermen had good visibility. We flew the client to boats to take measurements for the towers they would construct.

The "Left Sisters"

Besides flying for my air service and my membership in the Ninety-Nines, Bonnie and I were members of the Grasshoppers, a female organization of Florida pilots. (The husbands were known as the Locusts.) One event we took part in was a Halloween Fly-In. Participants dressed in all types of costumes from Raggedy Ann to ballerina tutus. Bonnie and I went as the Left Sisters, Orvina and Wilma, as a spoof on Orville and Wilbur Wright. We took my mother along as well.Flying with this group was all about the fun events, a welcome change of pace from our racing competitions.

* * *

1982 Air Race Classic

As the summer of 1982 rolled around, Bonnie and I were excited about flying in the Air Race Classic. Bonnie had raced in a couple other races without me and placed first in both. Maybe this race together would give us a first-place finish as mother and daughter. We would start in Sunriver, Oregon and finish in Knoxville, Tennessee at the World's Fair.

As we normally did, Bonnie and I flew the race route backwards. On the way to the starting line, the race committee asked us to tape some TV interviews for publicity when we were in Knoxville, Tennessee and Lincoln, Nebraska.

One night after we checked in at a hotel in Nashville, Bonnie said, "Mom, I have something to tell you. Laird and I are getting a divorce."

This didn't come as a surprise. Several years earlier I got a phone call from Bonnie that shook me to the core. Her marriage was in trouble, and I had to do something. I didn't have my own airplane at the time, so I asked a pilot friend to fly me up from Ft. Lauderdale to see Bonnie.

I always said I would cut off my right arm before I would interfere in my children's lives. Bob would joke, "You're slicing it like bologna then!" This time was no joke, and I hoped I could say something that would help salvage the marriage. "You're both adults. I can't decide things for you, but I'm here for my grandchildren." It seemed to diffuse the problem, and they stayed together.

However, in the years since that intervention the marriage had deteriorated, and I agreed with Bonnie's decision. I hurt for my daughter and her family, and I prayed that her heart would soon heal. We carried on with life, and flying was a big part of that for both Bonnie and me.

We resumed our pre-race trip flying across the country. I saw something in the distance that reminded me of the opening scene of the Walt Disney World TV program. "What's that ahead of us?" I asked Bonnie.

"That's the Grand Tetons," Bonnie answered. The rugged beauty of the mountains took my breath away as I circled around Jackson Lake and landed at the Jackson, Wyoming airport. This is one of only two airports in the country located within the boundaries of a National Park. The area, normally referred to as Jackson Hole, is a

valley below the Grand Teton and the Gros Ventre Range. It was largely unsettled until fur traders hunted beaver there in the late 1800s.

Large archways made of elk antlers sit on the town square's four corners in Jackson. We donned cowboy hats and went horseback riding. The dry air made our eyes burn, so we bought some eyedrops and kept going. We rode a lift up the mountain and built a little snowman. After an overnight visit as tourists, we flew out of the Jackson Hole area ready to race over more of this spectacular beauty.

The race began in Sunriver, Oregon on June 25. From there we flew north to Coeur d'Alene, Idaho. Flying over the

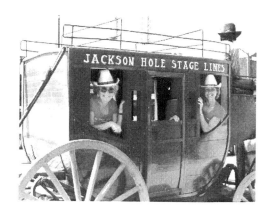

snow-covered Cascade Mountains with its craggy peaks felt like hovering over the mouth of Jaws. We flew over to Montana and down through South Dakota. We continued through the plain state of Nebraska, down south to Jefferson City, Missouri and Jackson, Tennessee. The last leg took us to Knoxville where we finished the race in fifth place. All the contestants received free passes and enjoyed VIP treatment at the World's Fair in celebration of the race.

New Beginnings

Bonnie's kids were growing up. David was attending Florida State, and Susan would soon leave the nest. Bonnie wanted her to confine the college search to schools within a 300-mile radius, or one tank of gas in her airplane. However, Susan wanted to attend Cornell University because of their Electrical Engineering program. Our son, Steven had graduated from Cornell with the same degree a few years earlier. Susan applied and was accepted.

When it was time to go, we loaded Susan's stuff in my van and drove her to school. Bonnie and I helped her get settled in her dorm room, and we slept in the van that night. Satisfied that Susan would be fine, we said goodbye and headed home.

Besides her children in college, more changes were in store for Bonnie following her divorce. One day she introduced us to Archie, a fellow pilot and friend she met when he took her instrument refresher course at the airport. Bonnie taught ground school, and she had been the Governor of the Southeast Section of the Ninety Nines. With so much of her life invested in aviation, we were happy she found someone with whom to share it.

In May of 1983 Bonnie and I entered the Shangri-La Grand Prix Air Race. Unlike our other races, this one included male pilots. The 2100-mile race covered fourteen states, starting

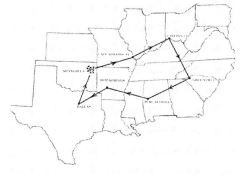

and ending in Alton, Oklahoma. When we flew into South Carolina for an overnight stop, Archie surprised Bonnie by flying up from Florida to meet us. I expected Archie would soon replace me as co-pilot flying with Bonnie.

Bonnie and I came in fifth place, and as always we sent out a note of thanks to our pilot friends following the race:

The land was water laden to the mighty Mississip.
The clouds in Cincinnati made us fly a zig zag trip.
The south was blessed with sunshine
Bathing pastorals we saw.
Then on we flew to friends anew
At windy Shangri La.

The engine hummed and nature strummed
Her tune as on we sped.
We thought of those below who wished
To be airborne instead
To share the joys of wings and skies
And hearts bent to the task.
We're glad to say "Well done."
And "Thanks to all" from first to last.

We agreed it was more fun racing with women because we could flaunt our outfits.

The Traveling Trampoline

In April 1981 NASA's newest manned vehicle, the Space Shuttle launched from the Kennedy Space Center. Following that successful mission, the shuttle launched every few months. People flocked to the Space Coast by car or motor home to witness the fiery rocket and hear the rumble as it passed through the clouds on its way into space. I joined our friends Betty and Bill in their motor home for a trip from Ft. Lauderdale up the coast of Florida to see a launch.

Bonnie and Archie Gann

Betty and I hit the store first to stock up on junk food. We partied all the way, and I had so much fun I told Bob, "We have to get one of these motor homes!"

I kept that in mind as we planned Bonnie and Archie's wedding for February of 1985. We held the ceremony with 100 guests in the great room of our Ft. Lauderdale home, a beautiful place to make a happy memory. A friend recommended a great caterer, and they spread a beautiful buffet on our large, custom-made dining room table.

224

With all three of our children living in or near Merritt Island, we wanted to spend more time with them. As much as we loved our home in Ft. Lauderdale, we decided it was time to sell and move. Bob put out a For Sale sign. A passing fisherman saw it and asked, "How much do you want?"

"A lot," Bob answered.

"How much?"

"A lot."

"How much is a lot?" the guy asked.

"Oh, $500,000," Bob said.

"Holy *&^=#!"

"We actually sold it for $400,000 to a society editor of the Ft. Lauderdale News. They lived a few canals from us and belonged to the Ft. Lauderdale Yacht Club. The wife had admired the house often, so as soon as it went up for sale, she told her husband, "If you're not going to buy it, I'll buy it myself." They invited us to visit whenever we were in town.

I met a lady at a tea whose friend was selling her home in Merritt Island. We checked it out and bought it, but rented it back to the sellers while we spent the summer in New York.

A few months later Bob and I purchased our first motor home, a Foretravel. We were about to enter a whole new world in vacation travel.

Bob and I planned a trip to Olcott just after the Memorial Day weekend. We assembled a tow dolly in Linda's front yard in 100-degree-heat. We pulled out of Merritt Island late in the afternoon on June 1, excited to begin our adventure. We by-passed sightseeing in St. Augustine and continued north because of the extreme heat. We hoped for cooler weather in Charleston, South Carolina, but it was still too oppressive for sightseeing.

Bob asked, "Honey, when do you think you want to drive?"

"Whenever you think you can handle sitting on the passenger side," I answered. From my perspective, it looked like we were going to go off the road and hit the lamp posts. Bob pulled over and we changed drivers. I think I only drove three or four blocks before Bob said, "Pull over." He understood what I meant, and he sure didn't like sitting in the passenger seat.

The next time I took a turn driving, I learned if I lined up the accelerator pedal with the dark spot on the road, it kept the big RV in the middle of the lane.

It wasn't long before we experienced the frustrations along with the joys of motor home travel. A problem developed with the water pump, and even after a call to the Foretravel dealer, Bob couldn't fix it. I envisioned hauling water jugs with us for washing and flushing. Not my idea of a vacation. Bob persevered though, finding a broken wire on the generator. He rigged up a temporary fix, and we were good to go.

We stayed in RV campgrounds along our route, enjoying local color and restaurant fare. A dip in the pool felt refreshing in the summer heat.

One afternoon our new air horn started to blow in spurts; then it died. We noticed we had no read outs for speed or engine instruments either. For the second time in a week we called the dealer about a problem.

Besides the mechanical troubles, we had to be aware of bridges and overpasses in rural areas because of clearance issues. Sometimes well-meaning friends suggested a certain route, not realizing that the motor home wouldn't fit through an overpass. We learned that lesson the hard way when we had to stop, unhitch the car from the towing rig, back up the motor home, and hook everything up again.

A few days after the horn incident, we discovered our jacking system didn't work. We considered cutting our trip short, but Bob worked on it and we kept going. On the busy expressway in Pennsylvania, we were driving along when the trailer tongue jumped off the ball and the car started fishtailing. A passing motorist alerted us. Fortunately Bob managed to pull over onto the wide shoulder and stop without mishap. We were so thankful no one was hurt. We had no major damage, just some torn electrical wires and a few bent brackets. A state trooper stopped to help, and we phoned for a tow car. We took an extra long lunch break to recover from the scary ordeal, then we continued on to our next campground. It was homey and pastoral with lots of animals around, but the roosters crowed all night.

Bob woke early, easy to do with those roosters crowing. "Honey," Bob said, "you stay in bed. I'll drive us to the dealer and we'll have breakfast."

I rolled over to catch a few more winks to make up for the rooster serenade. Every little bump sent me bouncing in the bed. The bed was all the way at the back of the motor home with its six-foot overhang. It felt more like a trampoline with every bump. The more I bounced, the harder I laughed. I laughed so hard my belly jiggled till it itched. So much for sleeping in. I got up and joined Bob up front.

The marks against this RV were growing. The last straw came as we drove up a long hill in Williamsburg, Pennsylvania. It would be more accurate to say we crept up the hill. The Foretravel kept losing speed. The speedometer read 19 mph, then 18, and on down. I was beginning to think I would have to get out and push. We even pulled into one of those truck emergency ramps to let the RV pant. Nothing helped. We didn't have the power we needed. How could we travel in real mountains out west if we couldn't make it up one hill? Before we arrived in Olcott, we were making plans to trade in this rolling trampoline.

Darth Vader's Cross Country

Bob wanted to replace the Foretravel with a Monaco. He heard they were the latest and greatest, so we flew out to Oregon for an RV show. We test drove one up a hill, and it passed muster, so we put in an order. When it was ready, the dealer called to tell us it was ready. He expected us to drive the Foretravel out there for our trade in. Bob told the guy, "You send a driver. This thing won't get out of it's own way. We're not driving it out there." The company sent two people to pick up the Foretravel, and we drove our car.

Helena, Montana was one of our stops on the way out west. We visited some friends there who suggested a route to Portland. We drove that leg of the trip at night and got a surprise the next morning. Our trailer was covered in black tar from the freshly-covered asphalt road. We were so disgusted. We had to get the tar off as quickly and carefully as possible. Bob found a hardware store where we purchased several cans of tar remover. We drenched the trailer with the smelly stuff in the parking lot of our hotel. With that mess cleaned up, we headed back to the highway.

When we pulled into the Monaco parking lot the morning of our anniversary, we saw our names on the marquee. Our anticipation grew as they gave us a tour of the factory. Finally we were escorted to our new motor home. The black and gray exterior and the huffy diesel engine made me think of a character from the Star Wars movies. We named it Darth Vader.

When I stepped inside it, I was shocked. The dinette, the Corian counters and all the trim in the galley was a burgundy color. "Where's the pretty green I ordered?" The dealer apologized, but there was nothing he could do about it.

Although it was our anniversary, I was too upset to be in the mood for romance. After a long talk with Bob and a good cry, I found a way to compromise. I asked Bob to find a paint store where I picked out a nice shade of green. I painted over all the burgundy in the motor home. Now the silk floral arrangement the kids sent for our anniversary matched. Bob remained placid through the situation. His only comment was, "Shirley, you're nuts."

It took a few days to complete paperwork, and we headed out to visit some friends in Seattle. This gave us a chance to let Darth Vader stretch his legs, and Bob to get used to driving it.

The new home on wheels had more room and comfort than our old one, and we were proud of it. Not only was Darth Vader an impressive sight, he had a horn that played several different tunes.

Once at a service station, three young people stood ogling the RV while I washed the windshield. The girl asked, "How many bedrooms does it have?"

"Just one," I answered.

"Really?" she said.

"Otherwise we wouldn't have room for the pool," I explained with a smile.

"You've got a pool in there?"

One of the guys nudged her. "She's joking," he said.

I'm always willing to tell a story just for fun.

Driving down the California coast offered beautiful scenery, but the drop offs were a bit scary. A few times the fog rolled in making the drive more daunting. I was glad to let Bob stay behind the wheel.

I got carried away cleaning at one of our stops. I cleaned the windshield, the side panels, and finished up with the wheels. Our new baby looked great, but I put a kink in my back. We tried to find a chiropractor with no success, so I spent the next several days lying on the couch.

Las Vegas

Ten days later my back was still on the mend, but the sights and sounds of the Las Vegas Strip helped take my mind off it. We purchased an RV lot in Las Vegas, allowing us to get discounts throughout the country at other parks. Our home base was an RV park adjacent to the Hacienda Hotel and Casino near Circus Circus in the heart of the city, and they provided shuttle bus service every 15 minutes. We ate at the forty-five-item dinner buffet for only $3.49 per person. We took in some shows including Seigfried and Roy with their beautiful lions and tigers. At $29.50 per ticket, it was the most expensive show we saw, but we thought it was fantastic. They didn't need scantily-clad showgirls to make it good either.

Between buffets and shows, I spent time in the RV icing my back with a package of frozen hamburger wrapped in a towel. Bob was afraid we were going to eat those hamburgers, so I told him, "Be thankful it's my back and not something else."

While we were in Vegas, Bob discovered a piece missing from the RV's tailpipe, so he called the dealer to ship us the part. He always found things to work on in the motor home, so one afternoon I decided to do some gambling on my own.

To say I was a novice was an understatement. I went into the casino and found a blackjack table with a dealer and no customers. I motioned to the $5 sign and said, "I don't know how to gamble and I can't afford $5. Can you change it to $2?" He complied. "I don't smoke," I added. "Can you take away these ashtrays?" Once I got comfortable, the dealer gave me some pointers. After awhile a couple came by.

"Oh look, it's a $2 table. Let's stop here," the wife said. Pretty soon the table filled up. I won about $20, and I think the dealer did okay too with all the people who came to play.

My back started feeling better, so one day we took a short drive to see the Hoover Dam. The enormous structure is amazing, and we learned about its construction on the tour. Later we took in an IMAX movie at Ceaser's Palace and I tried to win a car on a slot machine. I enjoyed Las Vegas so much—the fantastic glitter, the breathtaking scenery, and the inexpensive prices. There's nothing like doing Vegas in a luxury RV at $10 a night.

Arizona

We left the glitz of Vegas heading to the next stop on our schedule, the Grand Canyon. We enjoyed watching the changing scenery—first mountains, then arid flatlands with buttes and mesas jutting up. Gradually we saw some vegetation and piles of boulders. The Juniper Mountains were aptly named. The whole countryside is covered with juniper trees.

As we drove into the higher elevations, the trees changed and it turned cooler. We went from using the AC to turning on the heat. The elevation at Kaibab National Forest where we stayed was 7,000 feet. Even though it was cool, we didn't want to use too much of our propane. We decided to snuggle with an extra blanket. After watching a video on our VHS player, we turned in for the night. The coach rocked all night from the wind gusts. I never slept at a higher altitude than I'd flown. I wondered if it qualified for the Mile High Club.

We left the next morning and drove 60 miles to the south rim of the Grand Canyon and its spectacular view. We took a plane ride over the breathtaking scenery of the canyon. The co-pilot narrated as we flew around in the nineteen-passenger Vistaliner. The plane was equipped with large side windows for sightseeing, a great way to see the canyon. At times the pilot dipped below the rim.

Following our trip we heard about a terrible crash in the canyon by one of those planes. The temperature can vary by forty degrees, and the wind currents are much different below the rim, making it dangerous to fly. I think tourist flights were suspended for a while after that.

We visited friends in Flagstaff for a few days, but our schedule dictated that we press on to Texas. I nervously took a turn behind the wheel for a couple hours through some of the Texas terrain. It started out mostly flat then we drove through some rocky passes and long ribbons of road stretching as far as the eye could see. I gained experience maneuvering Darth Vader out of the parks and onto the highway, but Bob took it into the cities.

Texas to Georgia

Sightseeing in San Antonio brought back memories of a trip with Bonnie during one of our races. Bob and I saw the Alamo, took a boat ride, and strolled on the Riverwalk. The day ended with a ten-cent ride on a quaint replica of an old-fashioned trolley with beveled glass, oil lamps, and brass fixtures.

We left Texas and headed east traveling through Louisiana and crossing the Mississippi River. I thought about all the places we had seen since we crossed the river at the beginning of our trip. What a beautiful country we live in.

We drove through a lot of swampy areas, but I thought Louisiana was a pretty state. We planned to stop in Biloxi, but we forgot about Hurricane Elena that came through a month earlier. The category-three storm did a lot of damage in that area. Work crews came in to do repairs and stayed in RVs. We were lucky to get the last site at the park we found.

The next day we pulled out heading for Ft. Walton Beach, Florida. We stopped at a park for lunch, and I took a walk down the beach to the water. When we arrived at our campground, we called our grandson, Dave, who was attending Florida State. After a whole day with him, we continued on our way.

We were invited to lunch with Bonnie's mother-in-law in southwest Georgia. We pulled into the little town of Pelham and asked for directions. When I explained whose home we were looking for, the gas station attendant asked, "You lookin' for Miss Clara that drives a Cadillac?"

"That's right," I answered. He gave us directions and we found the lovely, rambling home nestled in fifteen acres of woods with its own pond. Clara was a tall, elegant lady, and she gave us a warm, Southern welcome. I could see how my son-in-law, Archie, became such a gentleman.

Clara ushered us down a hallway as wide as my dining room and into a comfortable sitting room. As we chatted with her, it became obvious she was a well-bred, well-traveled woman.

I wondered when our hostess would get up and fix lunch. Finally a uniformed black lady came and announced, "Luncheon is served."

Clara showed us to a formal dining room and a beautifully decorated table. A huge painting of Clara hung on one wall.

Two friendly maids served us from silver platters using silver tongs. We had melon and blueberry salad, roasted quail with wild rice, broiled tomatoes, fresh green beans, homemade biscuits and brown gravy. Our plates were garnished with apricots topped with fresh, grape jam. The meal was delicious, but Bob and I were uncomfortable with the gorgeous trappings before us. My tall glass of iced tea with its sprig of fresh mint sat sweating on the embroidered linen placemat. I felt self conscious about water marks on the lovely mahogany table. We managed to get through the meal and the maids brought out dessert. We each ate a generous helping of chocolate cream pie with meringue on top. Trying to make conversation, I commented, "Clara, this pie is delicious. What do you call it?"

"I call it chocolate pie," she answered.

"Oh."

I wanted to crawl under the table with embarrassment.

We visited a few more of our motor home friends in Florida before heading home to Merritt Island. They often wanted us to stay a few days longer, but we went on our way. I remarked to Bob, "It sure is nice to be liked and wanted."

We clicked off the last hundred miles of our six-week journey anxious to see our kids and grandkids in Florida. The trip to pick up the new motor home was a delightful experience, but we were glad to put Darth Vader to bed on his cement slab next to our house.

A sampling of the motor homes we owned.

It's All Greece to Me

We didn't have long to cool our heels in Florida. Soon we were packing our bags for a trip to Greece. Bonnie and I had won an air race and two tickets to anywhere in the world where TWA flew. We wanted to visit the family of Bonnie's Japanese exchange student, but TWA didn't fly to Japan. We settled on Greece and made plans for a trip in the fall. Something came up and Bonnie couldn't go, so she gave her ticket to Bob.

We flew from Florida to JFK International in New York City and took a connecting flight to Greece. The air traffic was backed up before take off, so we ended up sitting on the tarmac for a couple hours. I had convinced Bob we should upgrade to business class, so we had nice seats. However, when the man in front of me reclined his seat, I started to feel sick. I called the flight attendant who put me in another seat and gave me oxygen. It was much later when I discovered it was claustrophobia. Just knowing the reason the symptoms came on so suddenly gave me the ability to overcome it.

With my air race and motor home travels, I wasn't used to booking hotel reservations in advance. When we arrived in Greece, I realized my mistake. All the major hotels were booked, so we stayed at the Caravelle, a hotel often used by flight attendants. They had a room for us that night, but they were all booked for the weekend.

"What are we going to do until Monday?" I asked the desk clerk.

"Why don't you take a cruise?" he suggested.

We followed through with that idea and the next morning we boarded a ship to tour the islands. It seemed small by our standards, but we had a nice cabin with our own bathroom. The ship was going to the islands of Santorini, Rhodes, Crete, and Mikonos.

We saw the remains of the Colossus in Rhodes, one of the Seven Wonders of the World. On Crete we toured the beautiful ruins. I was amazed at the ancient flushing toilets dating between 2500-3500 B.C. Our guide explained that workers carried water up the hill from the river and dumped it from the roof into carved channels. Gravity did the rest.

Our favorite stop was the island of Santorini. Its crescent shaped vol-

Bob and I sitting on our . . . donkeys.

cano makes it recognizable from space. When we disembarked from the ship, we rode donkeys up the side of the mountain. I tried to keep my eyes on the wonderful view as the guide smacked the donkeys going up the steep steps.

Our stop during the cruise did not allow enough time, so after the cruise we flew back to Santorini for a few more days. We wanted to stay at the Atlantis hotel for it's picturesque view, but we didn't have a reservation. We asked the desk clerk if we could change our clothes and leave our luggage there. We rented some bicycles to tour the city and came back to the hotel around noon. The clerk informed us they found a room for us for the next two nights.

I loved the Greek food, stuffed grape leaves, mousakka, and yogurt and honey. They serve pound cake with yogurt and honey drizzled on top. The Greek yogurt in American stores today doesn't compare with the real thing. The flowers in Greece add a certain flavor to the honey.

When we booked our flight to Greece, I spent $700 upgrading our free tickets to business class. I promised Bob I wouldn't spend any more money. I could have kicked myself for that promise when I saw the 18 k gold jewelry in Santorini. Prices were fantastic. I saw a bracelet I loved with a leopard design. The eyes were made of emeralds and all the spots were precious stones. The price tag read $4,000, but the same bracelet would've sold for almost twice that in the U.S. I stuck to my promise and didn't buy the bracelet. There were only a few times in our married life that Bob wouldn't let me buy something, but I never let him forget that one.

Enjoying Our Family Circle

When Bob and I moved to Merritt Island, we parked our RV coach next to the house and lived in it while we redecorated. One day in the fall of 1985, Chrissie brought her boyfriend, John, over to meet us. After they left, I said to Bob, "Can you imagine? He's handsome and he owns a business."

Chris and John Condon

Chrissie met John at a Halloween party at his home and they hit it off right away. She dreamed of marrying a man who had property with a pond and some horses. She found the man with the property and pond, but the only horse she got was a wooden sawhorse.

On one of our trips I had bought a book titled, *How to Marry a Man in Ninety Days*, and I gave it to Chrissie as a joke. When we looked at the calendar later, Chrissie had done just that. They were married in February 1986, during a tornado watch. As the ceremony was about to start, John realized he forgot the marriage license. Bonnie's husband, Archie offered to go to John's office to retrieve the license. He missed most of the ceremony and came back drenched.

Zillig Movie Night

It was great living in close proximity to my daughters. With the advent of VHS rentals, we often invited them over for movie night. One night we invited Bonnie and Archie and Chrissie and John over. I made a sign for the front door, "Zillig Bijou," and created tickets with their names on them. The ironing board became the box office. We set up a table with concessions and drinks. I chose the 1973 movie, "A Touch of Class" with George Segal and Glenda Jackson. She won an Academy Award for her role.

"Are you sure you have the tape cued up?" Bob asked me.

"Yes. It's already in the machine."

I greeted all our guests and we sat down to chat for a few minutes. We dimmed the lights and turned on the movie. Suddenly the screen filled with a sight I couldn't believe. Ca-chung, ca-chung. The scene was a real close up of an x-rated movie. Even though the room was dark, I turned ten shades of red. Bob yelled, "Shirley, what did you do? Turn it off, turn it off!"

I was so embarrassed and flustered. All I could do was stand in front of the TV and spread the sleeves of my caftan wide to cover the screen. Everyone but Bob and I were laughing. My son-in-law, Archie had switched tapes when I wasn't looking. Our movie night had no *touch of class* that night, but the kids had a laugh on us.

Bob and I enjoyed our VHS player and video tapes at home or when we traveled in the motor home. In the 80s we bought another new gadget, a Commodore 64, one of the first personal computers on the market. It was about two inches thick with about a six-inch monitor. I was so proud of myself for moving with the times. Learning how to operate it was another matter. In spite of reading the manual multiple times, it continued to frustrate me. I later learned there was an error in the instructions, and I felt somewhat vindicated.

I signed up for a computer class and listened to the instructor talk about modems and bytes. During the break, the teacher asked how I liked the class so far. "I didn't understand a word you said." I was so out of my element that I just laughed. Eventually I learned enough to use the computer, and we upgraded as newer models came out. When the World Wide Web became available to everyone, I often struggled to get connections to my e-mail when we traveled. Now I can shop online or send e-mails any time I want on my laptop. It amazes me how people do that and more on their cell phones now.

Move to Forest Lakes

We enjoyed our motor home travel, but we had no place to keep it out of the weather at our Merritt Island home. We didn't have room to build a garage for it either.

Our son-in-law, John invited us to a home show where he had a display for his company, Toppertown. There were many vendors, and one of them was for the Forrest Lakes adult community. We told the salesman we might be interested, but asked if we could build a garage for our motor home next to the house. We got an okay, so we started making plans to sell our house and move.

We purchased two lots, one for the house, and one for the motor home. Then we went to Tampa to design our home. After it was delivered, we hired a builder to attach the garage. The builders made one wall two feet higher than it was supposed to be. The officials at Forest Lakes complained, so we rectified the mistake. After that, the board prohibited motor home garages in the subdivision.

* * *

As the years went by, more grandchildren were added to the family. Linda and Jack and their three children moved back to California for a time, but we lived close enough to Bonnie and Chrissie to babysit their children. When Chrissie's oldest child, Alex, was born, I watched him whenever I could. I kept my sewing machine in my large, walk-in closet, and it was large enough to put a crib mattress for Alex's naps and overnight stays.

Chrissie's dreams for her future included twin red-headed girls. She planned to name them Jessie Sue and Cassie Lee. She got her twin girls minus the red hair, and she did name them Cassie and Jessie.

When the twins were born, we were so excited. Bob and I drove our Bluebird motor home to the hospital to pick them up. We went to a park and popped some champagne to  celebrate the births. It reminded me of the story my parents told of my own trip home from the hospital in the new Pierce Arrow my grandparents purchased. I could identify with how proud they felt.

The girls looked so much alike, Chrissie put nail polish on one of the girls' toenails to keep track of who was who. One weekend when I was babysitting, I undressed them for their bath. I knew I shouldn't undress them at the same time so I wouldn't mix them up, but I forgot. By then the nail polish had worn off. I couldn't tell them apart and I started to panic. Then I remembered only one of them knew how to patty cake with me. I started playing with them, and sure enough one of the girls clapped along. I swooped Cassie up and labeled her with a fresh coat of nail polish on her little toenails.

I loved watching my grandchildren grow up. My granddaughter, Susan, nicknamed me Gramma Zoogie, and she wrote a sweet poem for my birthday one year.

Ode to Gramma Zoogie

I think that I shall never see
A Gramma great as Gramma Z.

Her motivation's 'bove the norm
See, what she wants, she takes by storm.

No rocking chair nor la-z-boy
Does grace her buns, nor give her joy.

But span the sky, orange wings upon
Or making tracks in Obi-wan.

She spreads her love and good advice.
You'll never have to ask her twice.

And always there when needed most,
Forgives you when you burn the toast.

All set to give, she asks for naught
So what she'll get cannot be bought.

This birthday for my Gramma Z
A heartfelt ode from lil' ole me.

Love, Susan--5/14/89

At this writing, I have thirteen grandchildren and eleven great grandchildren with hopes for many more.

I'm No Esther Williams

After we moved to Merritt Island, I often flew to Ft. Lauderdale to pick up my mother and Aunt Mae for a visit. Mother was naïve about things related to flying, like how much fuel I used. She'd offer me $20 and say, "Let us pay for your gas." She had no idea how many gallons we went through in an hour of flying, and I wasn't about to tell her.

The first time I took her up, she thought I was talking to her when I communicated with the tower. I would say something about my position and she would chime in, "That's okay. I see it. You keep flying." She didn't want anything to distract me from my flying.

Anytime I flew a guest in my airplane, I wanted them to be comfortable. Before taxiing out to the runway, I explained all the instruments in the cockpit. Then I would fly patterns and describe what I was doing in the air. I also enjoyed giving "penny-a-pound rides" for children from the Merritt Island Airport. What a thrill for the kids to fly over their homes.

Sometimes I would get permission to fly along the three-mile-long Shuttle Landing Facility (SLF) located on north Merritt Island. As long as I stayed 500 feet to the west of the runway, I was allowed to fly there. It was a treat for my passengers to see part of the space program first hand and take pictures of it.

Another thing I did for special friends that flew with me was to give them souvenir logbooks. I would have them do simple maneuvers, which I entered into the logbooks. They weren't legal logbooks, but they made nice keepsakes.

* * *

When Bonnie and Archie were married in 1985, he became her copilot. As a humorous way to pass on that responsibility, I wrote a list for my son-in-law.

The Air Race commandments

- As with a ship's captain . . . never say PLEASE.

- Copilot must wax, clean, and fuel the plane.

- Copilot must attend all race briefings, keep track of charts, registration papers, and luggage.

- During race, copilot must provide food and drink to pilot. Additionally, copilot must mop pilot's brow and shade pilot's eyes from the same.

- Pilot should not hesitate to read "Wall Street Journal" or movie magazines to pass the time while copilot is waxing plane and otherwise attending to menial race tasks.

- At hotels the pilot always gets choice of bed and other amenities.

- Pilot should take shower first to ensure having enough hot water.

- Copilot must do laundry.

- Pilots need plenty of sleep because of the mental strain. Copilots do not require sleep even if they are entitled to it.

- Most important of all, relax and take it easy; your predecessor set high standards for you to maintain. If copilot balks or gets surly, I am only a phone call away.

Passing the baton to Archie meant Bonnie and I spent less time flying together. My air racing days were drawing to a close,

so in 1989 when a new aircraft regulation came out, I made the difficult decision to sell my airplane.

I sat in the pilot seat of my Piper Cherokee hangared at the airport, my tears flowing freely. I thought about the thousands of miles I had flown in the little four-seater plane. So many good times racing all over the U.S., Canada, and Mexico with Bonnie. I enjoyed flying with Bob around Florida or up to New York. I flew this plane for ten years, the longest of the four I owned, and it performed the best.

The new direc-
tive required the wings
be checked for air-
planes that flew at low
altitudes. These planes
experienced hours of
jarring on the wings
and body of the air-
craft. Checking the
wings meant they would take them apart and look inside. Most
of the miles I logged during races, I flew as low as possible for
the best performance. This made my plane subject to the new
regulations. I wasn't about to fly it after someone took the wings
apart. Even though selling was a logical decision, I couldn't help
sobbing the day I sold it. I didn't know how I would adjust to
losing the hobby I so dearly loved. Bonnie still had an airplane,
and I could fly with her on occasion. I held onto those thoughts
as I climbed out of my airplane for the last time.

A few months after saying goodbye to my airplane, I took up another hobby—scuba diving. I had done some snorkeling in the Florida Keys when Bonnie lived there, and Bob and I took a crash course in scuba diving once on a cruise. It was enough for Bob to know he didn't like it, but it whet my appetite for more. Never mind that I was a sixty-four-year-old grandmother.

The first time I saw divers, I was an eight-year-old visiting my grandparents in St. Petersburg in 1932. We went to Tarpon Springs and watched the sponge divers don their cumbersome suits and put the heavy bell-like helmets on their heads. Heavy boots allowed them to the sink to the bottom, and oxygen came from a long tube attached to their helmets. I couldn't imagine how they could move around underwater, let alone harvest sponges.

Ten years later Jacques Cousteau and Emile Gagnan invented a respirator that allowed divers to carry tanks of compressed air on their backs. It was called SCUBA or Self-Contained Underwater Breathing Apparatus. Their invention revolutionized the field of diving, and it allowed even a senior adult like me to take up the sport of underwater diving. As a child watching the sponge divers, I never dreamed I would one day see the things they saw.

As I entered the pool for my first dive lesson, I thought about the Esther Williams movies of the 1940s and 50s. She looked like a ballerina wearing a perfect smile as she did flips and twirls in elaborate underwater routines. Bonnie and Linda had both done synchronized swimming in their teen years, but the closest I came to underwater dancing was sewing their costumes.

I wouldn't have to be graceful to scuba dive, but I had to learn the basics—how to put on my suit, vest, fins and mask. Once I mastered dressing for the sport, I had to learn how to breathe with a regulator, and most importantly, how to equalize pressure in my ears as I descended. It amazed me that an average swimmer like me could enter a whole new world.

There were six people in our dive class, but I was the only woman and the only person in my age bracket. My diving buddy was a nineteen-year-old, redheaded kid. One of the first things I learned was how to remove my mask underwater, put it back on, then clear it of all the water. When it was my turn to demonstrate the skill, the dive master motioned for me to take off my mask. I shook my head. *Uh uh.* He motioned to me again. *Uh uh*, I repeated with another head shake. The rest of my classmates waited patiently. Obviously I wasn't going to get out of this. I finally got up the courage to remove my mask, put it back on, and blow out the water with my nose. *This isn't so bad after all*, I thought.

The teacher played a game with us as we practiced clearing our masks. He would throw pennies in the water. The students had to find the coins and see how many we could put in our masks. I got so good at scrounging for pennies that I won the game.

One day we had to swim down to the bottom of the pool and take off our gear. That included the twenty-four pounds I wore to maintain neutral buoyancy. The next thing we had to do was swim to the surface and climb out of the pool. Everyone did the procedure without a hitch, but it wasn't so easy for me with my fluffy spare tire. I slapped my arms like a seal on the wet cement at the side of the pool, and then dug in my fingernails as

251

I tried to pull my tub-of-lard-grandma-body out of the water. *What happened to those muscles I used to have?* My young partner cheered me on. "Come on, buddy. You can do it!" The more I struggled, the harder I laughed. I laughed so hard I couldn't get out of the pool. I was the only one left in the water, and I felt like a frumpy walrus at Sea World. Eventually I made it out and back on my feet.

Once I mastered the basics in a pool, it was time for my first open water dive. Demonstrating dive procedures in the ocean was quite a bit different. We had five-foot seas to contend with when we had to take off the gear and swim to the surface. In addition to that, I had a watch to keep track of my time underwater and a compass so I knew where I was. I accidentally did a mask squeeze, and I noticed some blood. The pressure inside the mask gave me a nosebleed, but I didn't realize it until I surfaced. In my nervousness I bit the mouthpiece so hard I had to get a new snorkel.

The time spent learning new skills was worth it when I got my diving certification. My favorite place to dive was in the aqua waters of beautiful Saint Croix in the U.S. Virgin Islands. Our group did a dive at the site of an airplane wreck from a squadron that got lost in the Bermuda Triangle. It was so exhilarating to swim around the fuselage of the airplane with colorful tropical fish as companions.

When we were on a cruise to Tahiti with some business associates, I signed up to dive with them. We suited up and left the cruise ship in a little skiff. Our party consisted of a husband and wife, their twin girls, the dive master, and me. Everything was fine at first. We saw some beautiful sea life. Somebody in the group filmed me petting a Javanese eel. It had what looked like a plume of fine feathers on its head. Everything went south after that. The family and the dive master descended deeper, but I couldn't keep up with them. I tried to get their attention, but they were far below me. I swam to the surface and at first I couldn't locate our little boat. When I did, I pulled myself into it and waited, my anger rising by the moment.

When the rest of the group surfaced, they said, "Oh, there you are!"

I couldn't believe the lack of concern by the dive master. It was his job to keep watch of each and every diver. I felt his lack of attention endangered me, but I didn't tell Bob when I got back to the cruise ship because he would've raised the roof. I didn't want him to put an end to my diving either.

Each time I went scuba diving, Bob was happy to wait for me on the ship. He much preferred being *on* a boat rather than *under* one. Once again, he became an onlooker to his wife's hobby, but it just made me love him more.

Mildred's Birthday Adventure

My lovely mother approached her 90th birthday in the summer of 1992. My brother, Vern and his wife, Marlene and I planned a party for Mother at our summer home in Olcott, New York. I wrote Mother a letter offering choices for celebrating her birthday. "How about riding the rapids down the Colorado River or bungee jumping off the Brooklyn Bridge?" I wrote. The last option, "a family gathering," was the plan, but knowing Mom, she appreciated the joke.

Vern and Marlene visited Mom in Ft. Lauderdale and took her home with them to Merritt Island. Following an air race with Bonnie, I flew back to Florida to pack up my stuff and my Mother for a commercial flight to Buffalo. Bob picked us up and drove us to the cottage. I told Mom we planned to spoil her rotten for three weeks, and we did. We invited all our family and friends for a huge birthday party. It was no small task to keep all 90 candles lit on her cake. She surprised us by blowing them all out in one breath.

One day I took Mom shopping. She needed some shoes, and the closest store that had her orthopedic shoes was 30-miles away. Mom didn't make it easy to buy her things, and this time was no different. She always said, "I'll pay you back," whenever I wanted to buy her something.

"Why don't you use that $25 birthday check you got from your nephew, Ronnie," I suggested. She agreed, and I drove her to the shoe store.

"These are nice, Mom. What do you think?" She nodded, so I motioned to the clerk and gave her Mom's shoe size. Mom continued looking around. When the clerk came back with the shoes, I quickly got her attention and whispered, "No matter what these shoes cost, tell my mother they are $25."

Mother tried on the shoes and made a quick test run in the store aisle. "How much are they?"

The clerk stole a glance at me and answered, "$25."

"I'll take them," Mother said.

"Mom, why don't you let me buy you another pair? It is your birthday," I offered. "Do you see any others you like?"

"All right, but I'll pay you back," Mother said. She tried on another pair. "How much are these?"

"$25," the clerk answered. I watched for any hint of deceit, but the clerk wore a great poker face.

"Great. I'll take this pair too," Mother said.

"Mom, I can use my credit card to pay for this. You give me your birthday money since it's an out-of-state-check, and I'll cash it for you. You can pay me back later."

"Ok," Mom agreed.

I paid for the shoes and we left. When we got home, I wrote on the chalkboard in the kitchen, "Mom owes me $25." I knew she would be satisfied seeing the IOU in plain sight. Every day I changed the amount and Mom never caught on. At the end of her vacation, the IOU read $0. I cashed her birthday check and gave her the $25. She was none the wiser, and she believed she paid for the shoes with her birthday money.

Another thing we did with Mom was to take her on a tour of the Jiffy-Tite building. Our son, Steven, took over the business when we retired, and he was doing a great job. He proudly showed us around the factory and introduced us to some of his employees. When we were back in his office, Mom asked, "Steven, do you have to pay all these people?"

"Yes, Grandma, I do," he answered.

"Well, I'd get rid of some of them if I were you."

Mom was always saying something funny or strange. We took her with us to a wrestling match once, and she made loud comments about one of the wrestlers that made me want to disown her. "Watch out! He's got something in his pants," she warned. "He's taking it out."

The wrestler had a little bag of salt in his waistband. He would rub his fingers on it to irritate his opponent's eyes. Mother's comment conjured up a totally different picture. I told her, "If I take you again, you'll have to sit on the other side of the ring."

One year as we opened Christmas gifts, I got all excited when I saw a big box. As I ripped the paper off, I exclaimed, "It's just what I wanted!"

"What is it?" Mother asked.

"It's a copy machine."

"You people give such strange gifts," Mom said shaking her head.

After Mom's big birthday party we took a day to drive around the Buffalo area to all the homes we lived in when I was growing up. I marveled at how she remembered the dates and addresses. I took a picture of Mother in front of each one. I developed the pictures along with all the party photos and put together a birthday album for her.

Our time together ended all too soon. I put Mother on a plane to Florida asking the flight attendants to take special care of her. They did such a wonderful job, I wrote a letter of thanks to American Airlines. Ms. Duncan, a staff assistant in their executive office, wrote back. "Your letter was a special treat. Probably the most pleasant part of my responsibilities at American is to receive compliments from our customers. I have passed along your kind words about the caring service your mother received to our Manager of Flight Services. Please give your mother a birthday hug for me!"

I don't know if I'll be around for my 90th birthday, but if I am, I hope to have as much fun as my mother did on hers.

My mother, Mildred Altmann Henry, proudly holding her great grand twins, Cassie and Jessie, 1991.

Trading in Her Wings

Bonnie and her husband, Archie were scheduled for a meeting of the Florida Air Race Pilot's Association in January 1993. I flew with them in their twin-engine Beech Baron arriving on Walker's Cay, the northern-most island of the Bahamas on a Thursday night. We were there to set up a treasure-hunt air race planned several months in the future. On Friday we flew out to take photographs of landmarks to use for clues for the contestants. By 3:30 in the afternoon, we were at Rock Sound, down in the Eleutheras.

"Should we do any more today, Mom?" Bonnie asked.

"No, we have to be back by 5:00 for the banquet, so let's call it a day."

About 25 planes had flown in for the event, and we enjoyed fellowshipping with other pilot friends.

The next morning we were in a hurry to get back to Walker's Cay. Bonnie and Archie planned to go to Marsh Harbor to get some fuel first. They probably had enough for our trip home, but they wanted to fill up. I waited for them in my hotel room.

A short time after they left, someone knocked on my door. When I opened it, two friends from our flying club stood there. Their faces told me something was terribly wrong. "There's been an accident, Shirley. I'm so sorry," one of them said.

Bonnie and Archie's plane had crashed during take off, killing them both. A couple Bahamians saw the accident, along with the son of one of our pilot friends who was out fishing. They dove in the water to look for survivors. One young man thought it might be his mother, because Bonnie's hair was the same color as his mother's. They pulled Bonnie and Archie out of the water, but it was too late for life-saving procedures. My precious daughter was gone.

We didn't know why the plane crashed, but we estimated they were only at 125 feet when things went wrong. From the position of the right propeller, it appeared the right engine quit. They had no time for emergency procedures. Hitting the water from that altitude would be like hitting a brick wall.

I could have been on the plane with them that morning. Instead I was identifying their bodies. I called Bob to tell him what happened. "Do you want me to fly over there?" he asked.

"No," I replied. "There is nothing you can do. I'll handle things."

That's what I did—handle things. Like I did for my father's funeral, my uncle's, and my grandmother's. I did what needed to be done. In fact, my friends said I comforted the others in our group. My emotions were numb at first as I tended to the necessary arrangements.

The first thing I did was to ask the medical examiner to do an autopsy. I knew the insurance companies would need it to settle Bonnie and Archie's estates. This was a second marriage for both of them, and together they had a total of seven children. The youngest ones were sixteen years old.

The Bahamians were so wonderful to me during that time. Wherever I went, people hugged me—the driver that took me to the police station, the undertaker, and people in the hotel. I went to a boutique to buy a black dress. I'll never forget the shop's owner, Queenie. She heard about the accident on a radio report. When I mentioned I needed a black dress, she knew the reason. She hugged me for several minutes and spoke a beautiful, comforting prayer over me.

It took about a week to complete the necessary paperwork. I chartered a nine-passenger Navajo plane and hired a pilot to fly Bonnie and Archie's bodies home. The pilot knew them both, and the co-pilot was one of Bonnie's former students. We flew out of Nassau on a terrible, stormy morning, the weather reflecting the tragedy we had experienced.

We deplaned at the Ft. Pierce airport to go through customs. I panicked when I realized the authorities wanted to check to make sure we weren't smuggling anything. "Don't you dare touch their bodies," I said. It must have been obvious to the customs people that I was in mourning, and they left us alone after that.

Even though I had so much on my mind, my experience as a pilot kicked in as I gave Bob our estimated arrival time before take off. We did our final approach to the Merritt Island Airport at 2:00 p.m., the exact time I predicted.

I'll never forget the sight of two hearses waiting as we touched down. I brought my beloved Bonnie home to the airport where she spent thousands of hours training other pilots. Bonnie and I took off and returned to this runway countless times. This would be her last touchdown on earth.

A few weeks later we held a memorial service for Bonnie at the airport. I couldn't bring myself to wear black that day because we were celebrating Bonnie's life. I chose a beautiful, turquoise pantsuit, and I stood in front of the mirror in our motor home doing a final check on my hair and make up.

At that moment I had a vision of Bonnie's plane. The top of the plane was gone, and Archie was sitting in the left pilot seat. He rose up and took Bonnie's hand. "Come my dear." He often said those words to her. Bonnie reached up and took Archie's hand. They smiled at each other and went up hand in hand. They lived together, they loved together, and they died together. The vision of their departure comforted me that day, and continues to do so even now.

Our family and friends gathered at the Merritt Island Airport for Bonnie's memorial. We spoke of her wonderful life, we sang, and we prayed. Bonnie's daughter, Susan, who was expecting her first child, read a Scripture passage from Ecclesia-

stes. I shared my vision during the ceremony. At the end of it, we were instructed to go outside. Some of our pilot friends flew overhead in the missing-man formation, honoring Bonnie's years as a pilot. My daughter and friend traded in her earthly wings, and I will forever cherish her memory.

Golden Years

Adjusting to life without Bonnie was a strain on both Bob and I, but I think I felt it even more because of our partnership as pilots. I have a close relationship with all my children, but Bonnie and I shared the bond of flight. I missed her terribly, and nobody else understood that gaping hole. Bob and I clung to each other, and we comforted Bonnie's children in their loss.

The months following Bonnie's accident crawled by. Once the investigation was completed, we still didn't have much to go on as the cause. Bonnie and Archie were both experienced pilots. Bonnie had been a flight instructor for several years and had many ratings. The only thing we could think of was they were somehow using the auxiliary tanks instead of the mains. If that were the case, the engines would have starved during takeoff.

Everyone wanted an answer to the "why did this happen" question. We sent out a letter to our friends and relatives explaining what we could.

Life goes on, and the living must continue to live. Bonnie's first grandchild, our first great grandchild, Max was born a few months after Bonnie died. We took comfort in the new life entering our family.

Later that same year, Bob and I celebrated our fiftieth wedding anniversary. Ironically, we experienced a family tragedy prior to our twenty-fifth anniversary when my father died.

Just as we had done before, we went ahead with our celebration.

Steven, Linda, and Chrissie planned a big party at Salvatore's Italian Gardens in Depew, New York. We saw old neighbors and friends from way back. I was so busy greeting people I don't remember if I ate from the beautiful buffet. Bonnie and Archie were missed, but we celebrated as if they were there. I could hardly believe Bob and I had been together fifty years. He was as handsome as ever, and I felt so blessed to be his golden bride.

When we returned to Florida in September, we had another party and invited our Florida friends. People call retirement The Golden Years, but I could describe every one of our years together as golden.

We continued our motor home trips touring the country every fall. I felt like a turtle with my house on my back, and I loved it. We traded out our motor homes frequently for newer or better models, christening them by popping a bottle of champagne. Our friends teased us that we did it so often we should own stock in a vineyard.

It seemed I often had to be the one to pick up the new coach because Bob was sick. One such trip I went to Lakeland to get the motor home. I figured out where everything was on the dashboard, laid out my toll money and cell phone, and I was ready to go.

It was a real challenge maneuvering the 40-foot vehicle out of the parking lot and onto the highway. I pulled up in front of the house at my estimated time of arrival. Bob came out to see the new coach, but he didn't even feel well enough to climb up the steps to take a look.

I became a pretty good driver with all our travels. Bob loved driving, but he needed me as back up. On one trip Bob got sick while we were passing through Texas, and I had to drive from there to Jacksonville.

Another time I was at the wheel because Bob was recovering from gall bladder surgery. We were about twenty miles from home. As we crossed an intersection, a car came down the hill and didn't stop for the light. Bob yelled, "Hang on, it's going to hit us!" The vehicle rammed into the side of the motor home bouncing us around and damaging the door. When the fire department arrived, we couldn't get out because the door was jammed. They wanted Bob to climb out the back window. "Oh no you're not," I said to Bob. "You're not climbing through a window. You just had surgery." I don't remember if we waited for them to get the door open, but we did escape a little shook up. We heard the driver of the other car died the next day, and that he may have had a seizure behind the wheel. We were very thankful to walk away unharmed.

Bonnie inducted into the International Forest of Friendship in 1992.

During our annual trip in the fall of 1995, we stopped in Atchison, Kansas to visit the International Forest of Friendship. This 45-acre park was created as a joint Bicentennial project of the Ninety-Nines and the City of Atchison, Amelia Earhart's hometown. It honors those involved in aviation and space exploration. My heart felt heavy as we approached the park. I had dreamed of returning to this place. I was so proud the day Bonnie's

264

plaque was placed two years earlier. It was the last time we shared any time together. So many famous people have been honored with plaques at this beautiful place. We wanted to spread some of Bonnie's ashes, but forgot to bring them. Bob and I sat and reminisced in the impressive surroundings, and continued on our way.

A few weeks later, we spent the day at River City Products in San Antonio, Texas to get a new steering system for the RV. Mr. Dee Howard started the company after much success in the aviation industry. His most notable invention was the reverse thruster for fanjet engines. We didn't realize Mr. Howard restored antique cars and had a museum on the property. While we waited for the installation of the steering system, we went to see the cars.

We got an unexpected treat when we met Dee Howard in person. Mr. Howard gave us a private tour of his collection, and spent an hour talking cars with us. Bob thought he was in Heaven. Mr. Howard showed us photos of the multi-million dollar airplanes he designed and decorated for kings of oil countries. At the time he was designing a Packard race car for A.J. Foyt. Later that afternoon, Mr. Howard came by our motor home for a quick tour.

We took my mother on one of our motor home trips, and she was fascinated. "You have a nice place here," she said. Mother didn't understand that we stayed at different campgrounds along the way. "Where are those people we saw yesterday?" I explained they were hundreds of miles away by now. She didn't seem satisfied with my explanation.

As time went on, we weren't comfortable with my elderly mother living alone. She had no family living in Ft. Lauderdale after Aunt Mae died in 1986. As soon as we could talk her into it, we helped Mother sell the house and brought her to Olcott. "I'm going to stay with you," she said, "but don't change your schedule because of me. I'll be fine."

Mother enjoyed spending time at our summer home. She would sit at the bay window and look out at the water or play Yahtzee on the windowsill. She loved it when Bob took her sailing. To get her into and out of the boat, Bob put her in a boson's chair, a canvas seat held by ropes. The chair could swing over and be lowered into the boat. Bob was very gentle with her, but she became too frail for boating. After that she would gave him a cold stare whenever he left to go sailing. He felt so bad he quit sailing altogether while Mother was there.

Mom was such a people person. Everyday she would ask, "Is anybody coming over today?" Bob would come up with some reason to go out, and he'd say, "Come on, Mother. We have to go to the store."

"Oh thank God. We can get away from these four walls."

We never left Mother alone, but one week Bob had an eye doctor appointment that required an overnight stay in Cleveland. I explained to Mom we were going to take her to Steve and Barb's. I got her suitcase and started packing. I would put something in and she would take it out and put it back in her dresser. "All I get is moved from pillar to post, from pillar to post," she complained.

We finally got her belongings together and loaded the car. The thirty-mile drive was full of cold stares and silence. I was used to hearing Mom suck her teeth whenever she was going somewhere. It was a sign she was happy. She didn't suck her teeth once in that short trip. By the time we unloaded at Steven's and she greeted her great grandchildren, she was wearing her happy face once again.

The overnight stay wasn't necessary, so we drove home. I'm sure Mother was surprised when we came back early.

When we realized Mom's living arrangement wasn't working out, she stayed with my brother, Vernon and his wife. When Mom needed more care, we looked into nursing homes near our Florida home. I took her for a ride and stopped at The Arbors. Mom wasn't fooled. "What are we *really* doing here?" she asked.

The nursing home director came out and introduced herself. "Let me show you our flowers," she said as she steered Mom down the sidewalk.

It was so hard to place Mother in a nursing home. The day we moved her in, she kept asking me, "What are you doing to me, Shirley?" Bob couldn't handle it and left the room. While I was signing her in, my brother and his wife were discreetly moving Mother's clothes into her room.

I took the nurse aside and said, "If you want to make a hit with my mother, tell her how pretty she looks and compliment her outfit. She used to make all her own clothes, and she was proud of it."

That did the trick. The woman took Mother by the arm and walked to her room complimenting her all the way. Mother ate it up. She adjusted well making friends with everybody. The staff loved her too.

This wasn't the case with Bob's sister, Margie. She was already living there when Mom moved in. As gregarious as my mother was, Margie was just the opposite. Every morning, Mother greeted the day by getting dressed and tidying her room. She didn't understand why Margie stayed in bed for hours. "What's wrong, Margie? Are you sick?" Mom would ask. I told Mom she shouldn't ask Margie that, but my advice went unheeded.

One day while Bob and I were visiting Mom and Margie we shared a meal in the dining room. Our table was decorated with a paper centerpiece in the shape of a pineapple. "The pineapple is a sign of hospitality," I explained. "That's why you often see a pineapple on a welcome mat."

With a frown Margie asked, "What sign do you put out if you *don't* want people to feel welcome?"

We felt bad she had such a dismal outlook on life. Although she was ten years younger than Mother, Margie passed away first, in April of 1998. My mother was in her nineties and still squeezing everything she could from life.

While Bob and I were on our annual fall road trip in 1999, we heard Mother's health had taken a turn. We didn't have good phone reception, so it took a few days for the family to reach us with the news. *She's waiting for me*, I thought. We cut our trip short and returned home. Mother passed away two weeks later at the age of 97.

Entering a New Millennium

Born in 1902, my mother had lived almost a century. A few months after she passed away, we prepared to say goodbye to the twentieth century and enter a new millennium. There was a lot of talk about computers crashing on January 1, 2000, Y2K they called it. Some people expected chaos or worse, so they stockpiled food and other supplies. We didn't agree with all the doomsday predictions, but we wanted our family to be together as the clock struck midnight.

In an effort to "party like it's 1999," as the saying goes, we made reservations at some resort cottages in Kissimmee to welcome the new millennium. Linda and Jack, Chris and John, and Bob and I sat around till midnight to see what would happen. Nothing did, but we made more family memories.

The real milestone came a year later, on our anniversary to be exact. Bob and I were packed and ready to go to the Harbor Castle Hotel in Toronto to celebrate our fifty-eighth anniversary. Dan H, the man who did our renovations came by and asked, "Did you hear the news?" He explained what happened. In disbelief we turned on the TV and watched the surreal sight of the smoking twin towers the day of the 9/11 attack.

At first, we weren't sure what to do. It was too late to cancel our reservations, so we loaded up for the two-hour drive from Olcott to Toronto. We left at 10:00 a.m. but didn't arrive until 6:00 p.m. that night. Traffic crept along, bumper to bumper most of the way. The border crossing took much longer, the guards being extremely cautious with every vehicle. We were exhausted when we finally arrived in our room on the 25th floor overlooking the harbor.

The next day we did some sightseeing, tuning in occasionally to hear updates on the 9/11 tragedies. Thursday we went out in the morning for a while and came back to the room to relax. At about 4:00 in the afternoon, an announcement came over the PA system. "We have a problem. We would like everyone to go to the lobby. Please use the stairs."

My mind raced as Bob and I exited our room and joined other hotel guests in the stairwell. With each step downward, I thought about the victims in the twin towers. *Is this how they felt? Frightened? Panicked? I wonder what's happening here?*

We heard there was a fire on the 18th floor. By the time we reached that level, Bob was out of breath. We came out of the stairwell door not knowing what would greet us. Everything seemed fine. I called the front desk from a phone in the hallway. "My husband can't go any further," I explained as I panted. Walking down that many stairs took more energy than I thought, and we were frightened as well.

The desk clerk answered, "Stay where you are. The emergency is over. The elevators will be working again soon." I let out a sigh and told Bob the good news. When I looked out the window I saw the fire trucks leaving.

In a few more minutes, they told us we could take the elevator back to our floor. I felt we got a small taste of what the 9/11 victims experienced, and they were so much higher than we were on the 25th floor. It was scary and very sobering. From that day on, we never stayed higher than the fourth floor in a hotel.

* * *

A few years later, Bob and I wanted to move to a different subdivision, but there was no place to park an RV. At our age we weren't taking as many long trips anyway, so it was a good time to sell our last motor home. We weren't ready for rocking chairs just yet, so we opted for another form of vacation travel—riverboat cruising. I liked the idea of calm waters and beautiful scenery. The lavish amenities in the brochure beckoned us to relax and enjoy, and we booked an aft suite near the paddlewheel with two outside balconies for a weeklong trip on the Mississippi River.

Our 60th Wedding Anniversary photo, 2003

It felt like we had stepped back in time as we boarded the steamboat and settled into our room. Although the surroundings looked like a page out of the past, the ship had plenty of up-to-date entertainment and an abundance of delicious food. We could choose a restaurant on any of the ship's three decks, and everything was already paid for.

One day after we finished dinner, I told Bob I wanted to go to the purser's office, but he could wait for me. I left him sitting outside the restaurant. When I came back, I couldn't find

Bob. "Could you please help me?" I asked a steward. I explained that I couldn't find my husband and gave him a description of Bob.

"Why don't you let us do the looking?" the steward asked. Having some help made me feel a little less anxious, so I went back to our cabin to see if he was there. As I came down the hallway, there sat Bob, innocent as could be.

"I didn't want you to worry," Bob said. "So I decided to sit out here until you came back."

As it turned out, I was the one with the faulty memory. I forgot where I left him and panicked when I didn't see him sitting by the restaurant.

We loved the slower pace of this type of cruise. We were never affected by ocean storms and were always within sight of land. Bob and I enjoyed it so much we went on other riverboat cruises, up the Mississippi River, the Missouri River, and a southbound cruise from the Ohio River down into the Mississippi to New Orleans.

* * *

In the fall of 2004, Bob and I planned a trip to the West Coast of Canada. We drove to Toronto and boarded a train for the trip across Canada. Then we rented a car for a scenic drive on the Trans Canada Highway in Alberta on our way to Lake Louise. We spent a few hours in Jasper, Alberta sightseeing and shopping before continuing on our adventure. I smiled at Bob and remarked how much I liked the beautiful wool coats we bought there. It would be the only time we would wear them.

I was at the wheel and Bob rode shotgun. We were used to this set up with all the flying I did, and he enjoyed being my navigator. I was snug and happy driving along and looking at the picturesque snow-covered mountains.

I enjoyed the view so much that I missed our exit for Lake Louise, so I turned the car around and drove back looking for the turn. I noticed an oncoming car swerving erratically, and before I had time to respond, the vehicle slammed into us head on.

Other motorists had seen the car veering all over the road and witnessed the collision. One man pulled his car over and tried calling for help. Cell phone service on the remote highway was sketchy at best, so he walked down the road until the call went through. An ambulance took Bob and I to the hospital in Edmonton, but the two elderly people in the other car were killed instantly.

Bob had a broken arm, a concussion, and bruised ribs. My injuries were much more severe. Both legs were broken and the steering wheel had crushed my lungs.

In the hours following the accident, the Canadian Royal Mounted Police notified my family in Florida who were preparing for their second hurricane in a three-week period. Here is Chrissie's account of what happened:

It was during hurricane Frances that we heard of the terrible accident with Mom and Dad. John's sister Jennifer and her husband Phil were over watching TV with us because we had a generator that could run a fan and a few other things. It was Labor Day weekend.

The phone rang and it was a man from the Canadian Royal Mounted Police. At first I didn't believe him, but then I realized it wasn't a joke when he said my parents had been in a terrible accident. He told me Dad would be okay, but my Mother was in very critical shape in ICU in a coma and in an "iron lung" and may not make it through the night. I tried to reach Steve and Barb with no luck. We cried and prayed for Mom.

We went to bed that night with the storm brewing and the sound of the huge industrial fan that we had in our living room to keep the air stirring. As my parents had taught me through concept therapy, I pictured them being okay, healing, and my mother surviving the night. I gave her all my energy, power and healing love through thought and prayer.

Later that night I woke up to the sound of the fan, that mechanical whirring circular motion of sound. I had my arm in the air, circling with the sound of the fan. Somehow I felt that I was connected to my mother and helping her breathe in that mechanical lung through the night during her most critical time. I still believe that was a magical connection of healing.

Because of the huge storm, there were no flights out of Florida. I kept trying to reach Steve and Barb at all their numbers. Finally they called me back. They were in Toronto on the boat for Labor Day weekend and didn't have phone reception. Steve made immediate arrangements to fly directly from Toronto to Edmonton that day.

I have no memory of the impact or the time immediately following the accident. The doctor put me into an induced coma for four days. When I came to, tubes of all kinds were attached to me like so many tentacles. Machines around me blipped and hummed as they monitored every heartbeat and breath. A tube in my throat provided oxygen. Intravenous drips delivered fluids and pain medication. I faded in and out of consciousness, and I couldn't tell dreams from reality. At some point I went into surgery where they inserted a metal rod in each leg from the knees down. I was strung up with double casts and a tracheotomy. I felt like I had been run over by a Mack truck. I probably looked like it too.

One night while I was sleeping, I accidentally pulled out some of the tubes, so they restrained my hands to prevent it from happening again. A nurse came in to reinsert the tube down my throat. She got flustered when she couldn't get it the first couple tries. Then she jammed it in, damaging my esophagus.

I felt like a tormented prisoner in that hospital bed, and I mentally prayed with all my might. Many people were praying for us too. I knew if it wasn't for God, I would not have survived the accident. He gave me the strength to fight for my recovery.

Steve and Chris took turns traveling to Canada to be with us and help with our recovery, a total of four weeks. I'll never forget Steve's first visit to my hospital room. He came over to the bed and kissed every one of my toes.

At first I was very groggy from the pain medication, and the nurses thought I was too out of it to communicate. Chris knew better. She got a pad of paper and wrote the alphabet on it. I would point to the letters spelling out words and phrases and then Chris would tell the nurse what I wanted. Chris knew what a strong lady I was, and the nurses were finding that out, too.

When I could write on my own, they gave me a clipboard and a pen, but the pen wouldn't work because I was laying flat on my back. I kept thinking, *they can put a man on the moon, why can't they make a pen that will write upside down?* I used a pencil attached to the clipboard with a string.

One ray of sunshine eased my broken body. When I recovered enough, Chris wheeled Bob in to see me. He was confused and kept asking me what happened. I wrote notes explaining as best I could, although my memory didn't offer much. I wished I could lessen his anxiety. If anybody had to be this broken, I was glad it was me and not Bob.

I had the tracheotomy for weeks, which meant I also had a feeding tube. The only way I knew what I had to *eat* was the color of the IV bag—brown for chocolate and pink for strawberry.

I couldn't sit up straight in bed for weeks, but they tilted it at a forty-five degree angle. As my recovery progressed, they put me in a heavy, plastic brace and let me sit in a chair part of the day. I spent much of my time dreaming about what I would have to drink when the tracheotomy came out. Ice water sounded good, or maybe a milkshake. What flavor would I choose? After weeks of nothing by mouth, I hoped my taste buds would work again.

While Bob and I were healing, Steven worked on a plan to medevac us back to the states. It couldn't come soon enough for me. He booked a plane from Minneapolis to pick us up, cutting the cost of a round trip from Florida. Instead of a $40,000 price tag, the insurance would only have to cover $20,000 for the flight.

They wheeled me out of the hospital on a stretcher, and rolled it onto the jet. They had to remove some seats to accommodate the stretcher. It was higher than the windows bringing my head inches from the ceiling of the plane. Using my clipboard, I wrote a note asking the pilot to fly over Lake Louise and tip the wings so I could look out. He didn't do it, so I never saw it.

Bob and I both needed a nurse to attend to us for the long flight to Florida. She had to suction my throat every few minutes. I'd start to gurgle and I signaled to the nurse with my fist.

The plane stopped in Minneapolis to change flight crews, then continued flying south. I was glad to touch down in familiar territory, but we couldn't go home just yet.

Bob and I spent a week at Cape Canaveral Hospital. As soon as we arrived, they removed my trach tube. Unfortunately the milkshake I dreamed about would have to wait. The medical staff had to be sure I could swallow, so they hooked me up to an x-ray machine and asked me to swallow some thick, white stuff that would glow on the x-ray. With swallowing checked off my list, I could eat soft food and my strength began to return.

Steven checked me into a rehabilitation place in Melbourne to complete my recovery. I had lots of work to do before I could be released.

Soon I was strong enough to propel myself around in a wheelchair. I learned how to scoot my hips onto a slide board, a long piece of hard plastic used to help the patient get in and out of a wheelchair. I even practiced using the slide board to get into and out of a car.

I stayed about three weeks in rehab, and counted the hours until I could go home. I could eat mushy food, but I had to chew and swallow normal food before they released me from rehab. With all hurdles crossed, Steven and Chrissie came to escort me home.

Steven wheeled me to the front door of the facility beaming with pride. "Your limo awaits," he announced.

I barely contained my joy as they wheeled me out the door. I looked around but saw nothing resembling a limo. "Where's my limo?" I asked.

"This is it," Steven said as he opened the passenger door to a Mini Cooper covered with homemade signs. Steven and I sat up front, and Chrissie shared the backseat with the wheel-chair. It's amazing how we squeezed three adults and a wheel-chair into that tiny car.

They say laughter is good medicine. I could always count on Steven for a joke, and I was more than willing to take my medicine.

The transition to normal life at home came slowly. I used a slide board to transfer from here to there. The next step was to walk with crutches. It was frustrating at times.

When I was able to walk again, my right foot still gave me trouble. The heel was badly out of place, so I found an or-thopedic surgeon who said he could help me. He operated to repair the damaged bones. Many more weeks went by as I re-covered from that surgery and learned to walk on my new foot.

Years after that terrible accident, my voice remains for-ever changed to a deep, sultry tone, and I have nothing in the upper range. In other words, I can't scream or sing as a result of the tracheotomy and that nurse's rough hand. I can't complain too much since I was a dancer, not a singer, in my early days. My feet and legs work well enough for an active grandma, and my mind blocked out the most painful parts of the ordeal. Bob and I still had each other after a terrible car accident, and that was worth everything I endured.

Saying Goodbye

Bob and I were getting up in years, but we loved watching the grandchildren and great grandchildren grow up. Bob was almost 90 and as handsome as ever. I began to notice his forgetfulness, but I couldn't accept it. He didn't seem totally comfortable after we moved, probably due to the onset of dementia. I didn't want him to be embarrassed around people, so I compensated by helping him remember things.

One thing he never forgot was happy hour. He checked the clock and did a countdown, "Twenty minutes till happy hour," he would say. I think it was his way of holding on to his memory.

We celebrated Christmas of 2007 as we normally did, with our family together. I remembered the Christmas when Bob and I met. It didn't seem possible it was 64 years ago.

We weren't sailing a beautiful boat, flying in our plane, or traveling around in a fancy motor home, but we had each other. That was plenty to make me happy.

Following the car accident and my long recovery, Bob and I hired a helper to come in during the day. She did light cleaning, laundry, and anything else we needed. The kids were glad we had Dawn to help out.

Dawn put the Christmas decorations away as we marked the first week of the New Year, 2008. The afternoon of January 5th, she asked for some time off to get new tires for her car.

"Why don't you take Bob with you?" I suggested. "That way you will still be on the clock."

They left the house but didn't make it very far. As Dawn crossed an intersection, another vehicle came through and t-boned her car. It rolled and Dawn was thrown from the vehicle when her seatbelt broke. Bob's seatbelt held him in place, but he suffered some broken ribs. Both Dawn and Bob were transported to the hospital, and someone called to tell me what happened.

Chrissie and I both stayed with Bob in the hospital for several days. The hospital staff brought in a recliner that could unfold to a bed, but I didn't get much sleep. It was uncomfortable, and I was worried about Bob. He developed pneumonia as he laid in a coma. At times he seemed to rally, but after a couple weeks in the hospital he took a turn for the worse.

When his condition didn't improve, they moved Bob to the hospice floor. I held his hand and whispered to him, "Honey, they say the streets in Heaven are paved with gold. When you get there, send me a gold brick." It seemed a strange thing to say, but I guess it was my way of coping.

A man in a black robe and black hat came to Bob's room a few times. He bent down to listen to Bob's breathing, and then said, "He's not ready yet."

I didn't know the man, and his actions were unsettling. He seemed like death, himself coming to check on a candidate, and it made me very uncomfortable.

The third night on the hospice ward, the kids helped me with the uncomfortable chair bed. It wouldn't stay in the down position. Chrissie mothered me by plumping a pillow and tucking me in. At that same moment, Bob took his last breath and slipped away. The kids later said, "Dad probably didn't want you to spend another uncomfortable night in that chair, so he went on to Heaven." I would've slept in that awful chair the rest of my life to have Bob with me.

Steven put his arms around me to pull me from the room. I resisted because I didn't want to leave Bob alone.

My children thought their father's passing was for the best because of the dementia, but I didn't care if his mind wasn't so sharp. At least I could have held him.

In Loving Memory

Robert George Zillig

My memories of the next few days are pretty blurry. My children took care of the arrangements. Daughter-in-law, Barbie, wrote a beautiful poem, which she read at the memorial.

Always A Gentleman
by Barbara Zillig

Always a smile, open arms and a hug.
Always a gentleman

Imagining, dreaming, sailing under the sun,
Relaxing, reflecting, sailing under the stars.

Warm offshore breezes with moon-kissed waves,
Onshore cocktails looking over the harbor.
Always a gentleman.

Inventing, customizing, repairing and sharing.
Sailboats, trailers, motorhomes, motorboats.
Rhubarb pies, cream pies, apples and cherries.

Sparkling blue eyes and a crisp crew cut.
Good jokes and many laughs,
A natural, sweet disposition.

What an inspiration, what a gentleman.
I'll miss you Dad.

Bob was all that and so much more.

Dawn's injuries kept her in a wheelchair for some time, and she was staying with her aunt and uncle. She felt guilty for the accident, but I thought she was too young to bear the weight of it the rest of her life. I went to see her to offer some solace. I explained that in a way, the accident was a blessing because Bob's health was going downhill. The accident made it easier on him. Those words comforted Dawn.

I went home to begin the next chapter of my life as a widow. Whenever I faced a trial, I said, "God must think I'm strong enough to handle this." He had helped me through a lifetime, and I knew He would do so again.

Welcome to Paradise

Adjusting to life without Bob was difficult. Months went by, and I did my best to embrace my new life. After about six months living as a single woman, I decided I could use a makeover. Commercials showing the miraculous before and after pictures of beautiful women enticed me, so I scheduled a facelift. After surgery, I thought about suing for false advertising. I looked like a black and blue-bandaged pumpkin.

One day during my recovery, Chrissie came over to interview someone for my new assistant. In my post-operative misery, I was a bit grouchy. Chrissie figured anyone who could put up with me when I was in pain and couldn't have happy hour would make a wonderful assistant.

Having a helper every day was great, but after a couple years I didn't like being alone in my house at night. I talked to Chrissie about it, and we started looking at places where I could keep some of my independence, but I wouldn't be alone. Selling my home was no problem because my snowbird neighbors were renting and they wanted to buy it. They even took some of the furnishings.

When I toured Courtenay Springs Village, they had everything I wanted. I liked the three-bedroom apartment with screened-in balconies, and I felt warmth from the administrator and the tenants alike. One lady from our motor home club lived there, and she had good things to say about it, too. Ironically, my apartment building is close to the Merritt Island Airport where Bonnie and I flew for many years.

I chose an apartment on the top floor with a spectacular view of the Indian and Banana Rivers. I approached the venture of decorating my new home with great enthusiasm. I love Florida, so I chose a tropical theme. It took about a month to redo the floors and put in a new kitchen. While that work was being done, I set about filling the place with my favorite things, and ordering some *new* favorites. I kept my off-white dining room set, so I stayed with that color and ordered new furniture for the master and the guest bedroom. When Bob died, I started a collection of cute ceramic frogs. They reminded me that I had to kiss a lot of frogs before I met my prince.

Sprinkled throughout my apartment are pictures of Bob and me at various ages, one of me as a young professional dancer, and many family shots of the children and grandchildren. My favorite picture of Bob, Captain Nice, sits on a shelf in my living room where I can look at it and remember my sailor. A silk banana tree, complete with a monkey, sits in the corner.

My galley-style kitchen is big enough if I decide to cook, but my main meal of the day is in the common dining room where I can eat like I'm in a five-star restaurant.

I couldn't forget my knight, Max. The seven-foot tall suit of armor has been in every home since 1977. I placed him as a sentry in one corner of my bedroom.

In keeping with my tropical theme, I hung a little sign on the apartment door—Welcome to Paradise. My philosophy has always been to enjoy life and make paradise wherever I am. My sense of humor goes a long way in achieving that.

I've been known to tell a few tall tales just for fun. For instance, one day I went shopping for some new towels for my guest bedroom. My other ones disappeared between the wash and dry cycles in the eleventh-floor laundry room. As I placed the bright, blue towels on the conveyer belt, the clerk commented, "What pretty towels."

"Oh yes. I'm getting married on the 19th," I said.

"You are? Well congratulations. That's a beautiful diamond," the clerk gushed as she admired my ring.

"Thank you," I said. "We're going to honeymoon in Aruba," I continued.

"That will be nice."

"Yes, but he's old, so he probably won't last long," I said, finishing my story.

It was all I could do to stifle my laughter until I was out of the clerk's earshot. Moments of humor like that do more than a swig of Geritol for a mature, single woman like me. I figure, why not have fun as long as I'm not hurting anybody?

I take pleasure in the simple things. Besides pulling the leg of a store clerk, I like to shop online or catch up on e-mails, sometimes in the wee hours of the morning. Occasionally I hear the familiar drone of a single-engine plane coming in for a landing at the airport behind my building, and I remember my flying days. That's not the only thing I hear.

One night as I sat in my chair with the sliding door open, I heard the ruh, ruh, of an alligator and the response of a female. "You're out there with your mate," I scolded. "But I'm up here all alone." I knew they couldn't hear me, but I felt better.

When Christmas rolls around, my apartment looks like a Christmas catalog. The blow-up Santa sits in a corner of my living room. My front door decorations change with the seasons, and when the holidays are over, my "Welcome to Paradise" sign returns to its place.

I still dream about the traveling we did, flying around the world. At this stage of my life, though, I am content to sit in my little paradise. I love it, and I will stay here until they carry me out feet first. Until then, I have everything I need right here. I visit the second-floor beauty salon about once a week for my hair and nails. It is so comfortable to go to the appointment barefoot and wearing my bathrobe.

There are plenty of activities to fill my time. My friends meet once a week to play bridge, and we have movie nights and parties quite often for the residents. Last Halloween I won the costume contest.

I visit family and friends in California and New York occasionally. Last spring I went to Buffalo for my granddaughter, Heather's, wedding. Steven, the father of the bride, was worried

Dressed for one of our parties at Courtenay Springs Village

about the father/daughter dance. The day before the wedding, he and Heather came to my hotel room with a CD player.

"Mom, I have a favor to ask," Steven said. "I was going to take dancing lessons so I don't embarrass Heather, but I realized, my mother was a dance teacher! Will you show us a few steps?"

I chuckled as I taught them a simple box step, and they were ready for the dance in short order. I had come full circle. I started out dancing professionally as a young girl. Many years later I was teaching my son how to dance with his lovely daughter. Where had the time gone?

Bob and I made a wonderful life together for 64 years. We raised four children, became grandparents of thirteen and great grandparents of eleven. We built an empire literally from the basement up, working together every day. We shared a love that our friends envied. When times were hard, God gave me the strength to face it. When times were good, we

Steven and Heather on her wedding day.

gave thanks for what we had. No matter where life took me, I stayed on my pathway to paradise.

I am reminded of a line in my favorite Bette Davis movie, "Now Voyager." She turned to her leading man and said, "Don't let's ask for the moon. We have the stars." I feel like I've had the sun, moon, and stars all my life. I couldn't ask for more.

Jiffy-tite Today

During one of my trips to New York in recent years, Steven took me on a tour of the Jiffy-ttie facility in Lancaster, New York. I was in awe of the beautiful building, the automation, and the volume of production. The business moved into the

650,000 square foot plant in 1997 and opened a sales office in Novi, Michigan in 1999. The company opened up a new location for machining operations in Batavia, New York in 2004 and relocated to a larger facility in 2006.

More than 165,000 Jiffy-tite connectors are sold every day and delivered to six continents for over twenty brands of vehicles. At this writing, there are over 350,000,000 Jiffy-tite connectors in service. In 2013 Jiffy-tite marks its 50th year in business, and we project nearly a half billion Jiffy-tite parts in service around the world.

Our company has grown from a two-man "mom and pop" operation in our basement to a thriving business that employs almost 200 people in three locations. And we can still

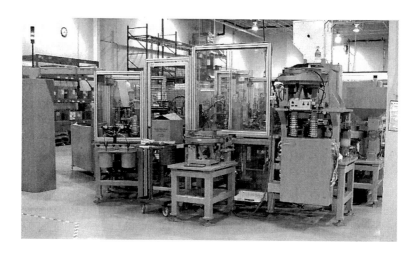

The main machine used in production at Jiffy-tite. It is called OSCAR, for **O**-ring **S**ealant **C**ap **A**utomated **R**etainer, a list of some of the components that go into a Jiffy-tite connector.

proudly say our product is "Made in America."

In addition to tremendous growth in the company, Jiffy-tite has won a long list of awards including recognition for extraordinary achievement and contributions to the economy

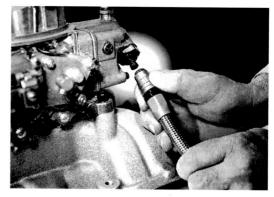

A Jiffy-tite connector being applied

of Western New York, finalist in Upstate New York Entrepreneur of the Year for 1996 and awards for excellence in business practices. Jiffy-tite has also received recognition for its support of several charitable and community organizations.

Steven had a special plaque made honoring his father and planted an evergreen tree next to it on the Jiffy-tite property. The plaque reads:

This tree was planted in memory of Robert George Zillig (1918-2008). Robert had an idea, design and plenty of dedication. After many years of hard work, Jiffy-tite company, Inc. was born. To this day, Jiffy-tite connectors are made based on his original design.

Epilogue

Following the writing of my book, my health issues became such that I needed more assistance. It required a move to a different facility and some down sizing. I am adjusting to my surroundings and making new friends. My "Welcome to Paradise" sign still hangs on my door, and I am thankful I can enjoy life wherever I am.

About the Author

Shirley Zillig has been on a pathway to paradise all her life. Raised during the Great Depression, she never let hardship stand in her way. She became a professional dancer at the tender age of eleven. During World War II, she met and married the man of her dreams, Robert Zillig. Together they formed a partnership in life and in business.

Bob and Shirley shared an entrepreneurial spirit, starting businesses delivering eggs and homemade bleach. Shirley took care of their four children while helping out in their businesses, and she even taught dance lessons for a time. When Bob came up with a quick disconnect gadget in his basement office in 1963, Shirley worked alongside him to launch Jiffy-tite. The company grew and in 1985, they turned over the reins to their son, Steve Zillig. Today the business employees almost 200 people producing over 165,000 parts a day.

In addition to Bob and Shirley's business partnership, they shared a passion for cars, sailing and motor homing. When Shirley took up flying at the age of 50 and started racing airplanes with daughter, Bonnie, Bob willingly supported Shirley's habit.

Bob and Shirley celebrated 64 years together full of laughter as well as tears, but they always enjoyed the journey.

Today Shirley lives in a wonderful assisted living retirement community and she daily counts her blessings. Her contagious zest for life inspires everyone she meets.